Time to Return
Law and Order
to the
American People

Time to Return
Law and Order
to the American People

Dr. Richard A. Vargus

Red Engine Press
Fort Smith, Arkansas

Library of Congress Control Number: 2024953118

ISBN: 979-8-9895620-6-0 (softcover)

Cover designed by Joyce Faulkner

Views Expressed Disclaimer

Subjects, thoughts, opinions, and even presentation of facts within this work reflect only the author's views and not the wider views of the publisher.

RED ENGINE
PRESS

Dedication

This book is dedicated to the men and women of law enforcement, heroes all, that I have had the distinct opportunity to serve beside throughout a lifetime of selfless service.

They don their uniforms and patrol the streets with one hand tied behind their back. Regardless of the political climate, they go forth to protect and serve with the knowledge that they must deal with two threats: criminals who are a threat to the community, and politicians who use the police as their scapegoats and pawns to project their personal and political agendas.

Be Safe

Saint Michael the Archangel Defend us in Battle.
Be our protection against the wickedness and snares of the devil
May God rebuke him, we humbly pray
And do thou, O Prince of the Heavenly Host
By the power of God, cast into hell Satan
And all evil spirits who wander through the world
Seeking the ruin of Souls. AMEN

Prayer to Saint Michael the Archangel, the patron saint for policemen and military servicemen.

Introduction

In 2019 I completed my Doctorate in Public Administration. I pondered my dissertation topic. I lived in a unique era of law enforcement. I saw firsthand the transition of New York City (NYC) in the 1990s. Once ravaged by crime and drugs, the city returned to a period of tranquility and safety with leadership and strong policing. Under Mayor Dinkins, a new police strategy came to the forefront. It was the police practices of Zero Tolerance and Stop Question and Frisk (SQF) that invigorated the reduction of minor crimes and provided police the ability to search for guns under the authority of probable suspicion. That torch was passed to the administration of Mayor Rudolph Guiliani whose legacy in crime reduction I refer to as the *Guiliani Stop Question and Frisk* era.

With the controversy of racially disproportionate use of SQF, I wanted to investigate if SQF was a tool to harass and target communities of color or was it an effective police tool. To do this I would frame my research in the only way that I could attain unbiased evidence. Evaluating SQF from the perspective of minority officers. I explored SQF from their perceptions. Each officer served during the life cycle of the SQF era (1995-2014).

The conclusion from this exceedingly small segment of minority officers... that SQF *probable suspicion searches* were effective in reducing violent crime. They also confirmed the impact of changing SQF from a sound police *tool* enforced by officers in the field to a politically directed quota system led to the racial turmoil. The common denominator that changed effective policing to a numbers game was... *politicians*. Has anything changed in the current chaos and uncontrolled violent crime surge that is plaguing this country?

SQF was centered around the *Broken Windows* theory and was adopted across the nation by other large urban police departments, such as, Los Angeles, Washington, D.C. and Chicago. The result... violent crimes, including homicides, fell fifty percent during the 1990s to 2010. This phenomenon is referred to by sociologists as the *Great American Crime Decline*. Police departments were aggressively tackling crime and enforcing violations for quality-of-life crimes. They engaged in disorder policing[1] and other tactics during the early 1990s.

Statistics provided from several criminal statistics sources; the Bureau of Justice Statistics (BJS) and the National Crime Victimization Survey (NCVS) codified this phenomenon. In 2010, BJS announced that during the period 1990-2000 crime had reached a four-decade low. The NCVS in September 2002 reported violent crime rates for murder and manslaughter dropped by more than fifty percent during that same period.[2]

Now, with the impact of *defund the police* and *no cash bail*, is the country in a criminal downward spiral? Is this the same spiral we experienced during the crack cocaine epidemic of the 1980s... an exact replica of the epidemic or even worse? Crack cocaine has been replaced

---

[1] crimesolutions.ojp.gov/ratedpractices/disorder-policing
[2] https://bjs.ojp.gov/content/pub/pdf/cv01.pdf#:~:text=Between%201993%20and%202001%20the%20
violent%20crime%20rate,65%25%2C%20and%20the%20property

by fentanyl, funneled across the border by illegal aliens and cartels. Deaths from this poison have exceeded one hundred thousand and continues to increase. During the Biden administration known terrorists calmly walked across our border and were released without vetting. Anti-American protesters are spewing the destruction of this country on our college campuses. Violent crime is at its highest levels in thirty years.

A government of the people has the responsibility to maintain law and order. Societal and physical disorder is a precursor to more serious crime. Communities live in fear. Crime ravaging their communities. While politicians hide behind manipulated statistic, do not live in these criminally impacted neighborhoods, and travel with their protective details. Is a transition on the horizon? Addressing disorder has become a central fixture of policing, especially in the United States' urban centers.

The effectiveness of disorder policing strategies in controlling crime has remained split along racial lines. Policing disorderly conditions can be divided into two main strategies:

a) Order maintenance or zero tolerance. This is policing that includes SQF, where police attempt to impose order through strict enforcement.
b) community policing and problem-solving. This is where police attempt to produce order and reduce crime through cooperation with community members and by addressing specific recurring problems. The inclusion of violence interrupters, who have cost millions in New York and Washington D.C., yet no statistics are available to show any evidence that these former "violent felons" have had "influence" in reducing crime. A failed program, change to crime in underserved communities… Zero.

Community and problem-oriented policing are characterized by police efforts to engage the cooperation of the community. Addressing societal disorder and physical conditions are police strategies based on the specific crime trends in a specific community/precinct. Unfortunately, strategic disorder policing has all but vanished.

The explosion of crime is occurring in NYC, Chicago, Atlanta, New Orleans, Portland and Los Angeles, where violent crime has shown increases from twenty-two percent to thirty-five percent. What we have seen is the reverse of disorder policing. Now communities are functioning in total disorder, without effective or efficient policing. The police are being hampered by restrictive policies. Policing is no longer a reputable profession. The manipulation of the new ideology of *defunding the police* is leaving departments with limited resources. The negativity towards police and the *Ferguson effect* are furthering the enforcement divide. Failed policies and lax laws are allowing criminals to evade prosecution. The system is empowering criminals, with more rights than law abiding citizens.

It's up to *We the People* of every race and ethnicity to decide the fate of the nation.

As you read the book, you do the analysis. It is the citizens, not the politicians, that have the power to determine public safety in the United States of America.

The Controversy

The impressive drop in crime from 1990 to 2009 are credited to the internal restructuring of the NYPD. SQF and Zero Tolerance are directly related to the crime drop in NYC. The FBI's Uniform Crime Report (UCR) database showed reductions in major crimes, including both violent and property crimes. The overall reduction ranged from sixty-three percent to ninety-four percent.[3]

The magnitude of the decline in NYC was represented by the dramatic decrease in each of the seven most violent offenses. These are called "index crimes"[4] – murder and non-negligent manslaughter, forcible rape, robbery, aggravated assault, burglary, larceny (theft), motor vehicle theft. Four of the seven – murder, robberies, burglaries, and car theft, showed declines ranging from seventy-five to eighty percent.

Supporters of the NYPD's strategies claimed that policing tactics, such as order maintenance programs and SQF, were directly linked and are the primary reason of the significant reduction in crime. The reductions in crime were reported to be about twice the national average. Analysis of NYC stops was rarely neutral or benign. Members of the community voiced complaints that they were treated with indignity, verbal and physical force. Physical contact was reported in twenty-three percent of stops, and three percent of encounters resulted in handcuffs. Even though the level of suspicion did not warrant it, frisks occurred in thirty-eight percent of SQF encounters, and in twenty percent of stops. Police were more likely to draw a weapon against a Black suspect without regard to the initial reason for the stop.

The New York Civil Liberties Union (NYCLU) provided the opposite perspective of SQF. Their analysis in a report dated December 12, 2022, clearly presented SQF as a targeting practice against minorities. From 2003 through 2023, ninety percent of people stopped by the NYPD were people of color. Black and Latino New Yorkers made up fifty-two percent and thirty-one percent of all stops despite being twenty-three and twenty-nine percent of the population, respectively. White New Yorkers made up ten percent of stops though they represent thirty-three percent of the population. In two hundred ninety-seven of the cities' communities the results were consistent. The analysis revealed that Black males were more frequently stopped. The results supported data for that period from NYPD's application of criminology data (CompStat). In 2024 the crime data has not dramatically changed. Was CompStat and statistical analysis racist? The demographics of violent crime over the past twenty years remains consistent – centralized in minority neighborhoods. This is a disturbing trend that is applicable to other urban cities – Washington D.C., Baltimore, Chicago.

The argument depends on which side you align yourself – the American Civil Liberties Union (ACLU) or the NYPD. Either side will sway your opinion. Both sides relied on their analysis of available data. The data varied from one spectrum to the other. Affecting the controversy were legal perspectives, societal measures, crime rates and even healthcare. Each side relied on the credibility of their statistics. But the variables of their positions were skewed.

---

[3] Crime/Law Enforcement Stats (UCR Program) — FBI
[4] Index Crimes Law and Legal Definition | USLegal, Inc.

The police used criminal statistics, CompStat, as their measure of SQF effectiveness. The ACLU conducted surveys and interviews targeting only African Americans in the affected communities, inclusive of personal experiences, perspectives and opinions. The same statistics were framed to fit the desired political outcome.

But where are the platform changes with the analysis of community policing? Establishing trust and community engagement are not determined from a statistical measure of success. How the community and police develop trust and work together is dependent on compassion, desire, empathy and a unified team concept. That ethos has nothing to do with race. It is the community and police transforming from wary adversaries to be united in a common cause. Their efforts are to co-produce the Emmy award-winning production of *community public safety*. NYC remains the cultural melting pot of the universe. The NYPD has been the most focused department in the nation to evolve in their institutional, organizational and community acceptance of multiple cultures. Their acceptance to change is reflected in the diversity of the NYPD… fifty-three percent of their officers are of races other than white.[5] The department evolved as the city's ethnic population evolved, without government intervention. It evolved as the city did, through a natural progression.

Measuring success is impossible to achieve statistically. And there is a variable that prohibits analysis for a race conclusion of police/community partnerships. While the argument that NYPD solely targeted blacks, a single race analysis provides inaccurate information. It does not include the census of the city's residents. In a random sampling of race, it does not provide validity with the other ethnic and racial groups. This is a consideration that needs to be given equal weight in the presentation of conclusions.

SQF was initiated on probable suspicion of who to stop. Was it racial targeting? The openly admitted strategy of the NYPD to determine who to stop was based on three characteristics. The first and the most damning… demographics. Traits of young Black or Hispanic males were based on a pattern of criminal behavior. But that strategy was flawed. How do you determine criminal behavior vs. suspicious or evasive behavior?

A reactive behavior may simply be due to the presence of a police officer in proximity. This is not unique. It is a reflex behavior, a natural response based on *street mentality*. How did officers in the street separate these characteristics, determining who to stop?

What is fact is that the greatest decline in crime was in disadvantaged neighborhoods. African American and Hispanic communities across the country experienced crime reduction at a magnitude double that of the experience by white citizens. The massive reduction in crime was identified in the FBI's UCRs during the SQF era (1994-2014). The unfortunate trend is the demographics has not changed. The numbers are conclusive, the increases in criminal behavior, criminal sanctions and incarcerations remain disproportionate within underrepresented communities. What can be done? The multiple issues facing underrepresented communities comes full circle… back to politicians who make empty promises.

---

[5] Microsoft Power BI (powerbigov.us)

Contents

Tables

Chapter 1 – Legal Foundation

Challenges faced by police departments and law enforcement agencies in the U.S. are complex. Departments seek to develop effective strategies to reduce crime and the fear of crime. Their sworn task… to maintain civil order by balancing procedural justice in police practices safeguarding the respect of those served and preserving police legitimacy. The ultimate procedural guide is the *Constitution of the United States*. The judicial system provides oversight for legal interpretations.

I was surprised during my research that the premise of Stop Question and Frisk was first introduced in the common Law of England. Established in 1066.[6] Probable suspicion was included in the law to effect searches for stolen property. English constables and "watchmen" were permitted to detain "nightwalkers" … suspicious people encountered at night.

Stop Question and Frisk (SQF) was the legal interpretation of the Supreme Court decision in the 1968 ruling in *Terry vs. Ohio*. This ruling upheld the legal challenge of "*probable suspicion*" searches. The driver, Terry, legally allowed officers to search his vehicle. Officers suspected that he may have had a weapon. The Supreme Court ruled that the search based on the officer's "*suspicion*" did not violate the Constitution's Fourth Amendment of probable cause. This decision provided police officers constitutional discretionary authority "*based on their training and experience*" to legally execute probable suspicion stops. The authority extended not only to traffic stops, but individual citizens. Commonly referred to in the law enforcement community as *Terry Stops*.

The Court's findings in *Terry* expanded law enforcements' toolbox to reduce crime. New York State capitalized on *Terry vs. Ohio* decision, enacting New York *State Penal Law 140.50, Temporary Questioning of Persons in Public Places and the Search for Weapons*. This little-known section of the New York State penal law would serve as the legal authority to implement stop question and frisk. The law provides:

The legal authority for police to briefly interfere with a citizen's freedom of movement, question and if necessary, frisk a citizen when the officer believes that some criminal activity is, has or will occur. This authority also grants the officer the power to briefly frisk the person stopped, when the officer can articulate a reasonable suspicion that the person stopped might be armed or present a level of danger to the officer or the public.

What the law dictates is the procedures to affect a probable suspicion search:

1. **Temporary Questioning of Persons in Public Places**: A police officer, in addition to the authority provided for making an arrest without a warrant, may stop a person in a public place within their geographical area of employment if they had reasonable suspicion that the person is:
   a) Committing a felony, or
   b) Committing a misdemeanor defined in the penal law.

---

[6] https://doi.org/10.1093/oso/9780198812609.003.0001

The officer may then demand the person's name, address, and an explanation of their conduct. Similarly, any peace officer providing security services for a court of the unified court system may stop a person around the courthouse under similar circumstances.

2. **Search for Weapons**: When stopping a person as described above, if the police officer or court officer reasonably suspects that they are in danger of physical injury, they may search the person for a deadly weapon or any instrument, article, or substance readily capable of causing serious physical injury. This search is not typical and applies only when the officer believes the individual poses a threat. If such a weapon or instrument is found, the officer may either retain it until the completion of questioning or arrest the person.

3. **Recording Personal Identity Information**: In cities with a population of one million or more, information that establishes the personal identity of an individual who has been stopped, questioned, and/or frisked by a police officer or peace officer (such as name, address, or social security number) shall not be recorded in a computerized or electronic database if the individual is released without further legal action. However, generic characteristics like race and gender may still be included in such databases.

Remember that this law was aimed to balance public safety with individual rights, allowing officers to take necessary actions while *respecting privacy and civil liberties*. Officer discretion was the key element. A viable law enforcement "tool" to serve the community is the removal of guns from the street. The interviews from minority officers unanimously concurred that probable suspicion was an effective tool that took guns off the street… when they were allowed to execute *officer discretion*.

As we proceed with the legal framework it is important that the reader understand legal terms and references associated with Stop Question and Frisk:

Crime. "Any act that the government has declared to be contrary to the public good that is declared by statue to be a crime, and that is prosecuted in a criminal proceeding."

Fourth Amendment. The Constitutional guarantee that citizens have the right to security of their "persons, houses, papers, and effects, against unreasonable searches and seizures, shall not be violated" by unreasonable search or seizure. *The rule of Probable Cause*.

Furtive movements. Stealthy/shady movements during the stop, question, and frisk by a police officer.

Mayoral administration. The elected and appointed administrative body that performs public administration in the City of New York. The Mayoral Administration serves as the Executive Branch of NYC Government.

Police precinct/district/station/beat. The geographic headquarters and patrol area where police perform foot or vehicular patrols.

Reasonable suspicion. A police officer's belief, based on articulable facts, that criminal activity is afoot; reasonable suspicion allows for stop and frisks.

Search. The United States Supreme Court has defined a search as prying into that which is hidden. The Fourth Amendment prohibits an unreasonable search or seizure. Police officers are granted the authority to frisk the outer clothing of a person who has been lawfully stopped based on a reasonable and articulable fear that the person might be armed (*Terry vs. Ohio*, 392 U.S.C.).

Seizures. A seizure occurs when police officers use their authority to take a person or property into custody, thus stopping the person's freedom of movement and retaining custody of property until a formal or informal disposition can be made.

Stop. When a government official interferes with an individual's freedom of movement based on the officer's reasonable suspicion that criminal activity is afoot (*del Carmen*, 2010).

Terry v. Ohio (1968). The United States Supreme Court decision that granted legal basis for a police officer providing the authority to stop and frisk suspects when there is reasonable suspicion that a crime has been or is about to be committed (*del Carmen*, 2010).

UF-250 police report (NYPD). Stop, question, and frisk report used for documentation when a police officer stops, questions and frisks a person (*Jones-Brown, Gill, & Trone*, 2010).

Chapter 2 – Themes

The foundation of the book focuses around four themes. The themes are as valid today as during the stop question and frisk era. Today, history is repeating itself. Will citizens, the police and politicians generate stakeholder unity? Or will our nation remain on the path to alienate its citizens and deny us the protections promised by the constitution.

Themes	Assumptions
SQF – Success or Failure	It worked.
	It worked, BUT…
	It worked, but it was a numbers game.
	It was a failure.
License to Fish (CompStat)	That's not what CompStat said.
	It is political.
	There was a cost.
Race	Setting the Stage
	Biased Enforcement?
Community	Safety and Peace
	Involvement

Each of these themes will be explored. An unvarnished deep dive. There are no biased conclusions, just the facts, and sometimes the facts are hard to accept. One thing is quite clear. NYC, as the nation's most diverse metropolis, identified the need to restore public safety. For two decades the city was recognized as the safest in the nation. The themes are the pieces of the puzzle that present the story of one of the biggest policy successes to reduce crime in New York. And in so doing, revitalized its economy, infrastructure, virtue and the resiliency of New York City.

It's also a story of a city where political manipulation crucified the effectiveness of the police department. When the curtain of darkness rolled over New York and the urban cities across the country in 2020, we returned to the dark ages of public safety. Can we return to a balance of fair enforcement, safe streets, and the rule of law? With the spike driven into the heart of law enforcement, we may never be able to bridge that gap and return to resolute and effective policing. Are the police obsolete? Can social workers and violence interrupters maintain law and order? You, the people, must be the judge and jury.

Chapter 3 – The Fuse is Lit

The racial powder keg has been simmering for decades. It can be traced back to Rodney King's brutal beating by the Los Angeles Police on March 3, 1991. King's beating was captured on national television. Beaten by white officers, it sparked outrage in the Black Community, leading to days of riots in Los Angeles and across the country in minority communities. It forced public awareness of the disparate police enforcement tactics of minorities. It opened the eyes of elected officials, forcing awareness and the need for change in policing.

Amadou Diallo, a black Guinean student was killed in the Bronx on February 4, 1999. At 12:40 A.M., members of the NYPD Street Crimes Unit (SCU) engaged Diallo, who ran from police after being directed to stop. Diallo was confronted on the steps of his apartment and directed multiple times to turn around with his hands raised. He refused. Eventually turning to face the officers holding a black object that turned out to be his wallet. Officers opened fire. Forty-one rounds were fired, killing Diallo. The four officers were white. Charged with second degree murder, they were acquitted, sparking outrage in the Black community.

In Baltimore on April 12, 2015, a twenty-five-year-old Black man, Freddie Carlos Gray with an extensive criminal record, was arrested by the Baltimore Police Department for possession of a knife. During his arrest, Gray sustained injuries and was taken to R Adams Cowley Shock Trauma Center, where he died on April 19, 2015. His cause of death was described as a severe spinal cord injury. Allegations were levied against the arresting officers that they failed to properly secure him for transportation in the police van. Asserting officers' negligence directly related to the cause of Gray's death. His death sparked protests, looting and destruction of public and private property in the Black Baltimore community. Six officers, including three African American Officers, were indicted. Like the Rodney King case, all officers were eventually acquitted.

But this case was not the typical white cop vs. black perpetrator. The case was not racially motivated. The supervisor on duty was black as were two of the arresting officers. Regardless the black community and media had a field day professing police racism. Clamoring for justice. The same equation… police arrest plus black suspect equals systematic police racism. The standard that all police officers are racists was dispelled by the facts. Unfortunately, the media wanted sensationalism. And that's what they got, at the expense of frustrated minority residents. Turning to looting, rioting and destruction to release their frustrations. Today that Baltimore community remains in shambles. Poverty, unemployment, drugs, and violent crime rampant.

On July 17, 2014, Eric Garner, a forty-three-year-old African American engaged in an altercation for selling illegal cigarettes. When approached by officers he resisted arrest. In the ensuing struggle NYPD officers used what was determined to be a prohibited "choke hold" maneuver. Garner subsequently died from what was deemed suffocation, however underlying health conditions may have contributed to his death. Garner's death rallied support from the fledgling Black Live Matter movement, raising national attention of police involved disproportionate encounters with black suspects. The officers involved in the arrest were white.

Officers were acquitted but the officer executing the "choke hold" was brought up on departmental charges and terminated. The Garner family sued the department, settling for millions from the city in their wrongful death civil case.

Then the lid of racial injustice finally blew up, when George Floyd was killed in Minneapolis Minnesota on May 25, 2020. The Black Lives Matter organization rising from the depths of the national racial injustice call to arms. Their revolutionary tactics... fostering violence, anarchy and destruction of property. All in the name of racial justice. National protests demanding that the police be defunded, and massive changes in the criminal justice system. The question... has the rise of BLM, and the national outcry for racial justice changed anything? Have Urban cities across the nation seen a dramatic reduction of violent crime since 2020 or in the past thirty years? Have underrepresented communities experienced improvements in socio-economic conditions? The facts in this book are eye opening.

Clearly the economy has not improved, inflation punishing the working class. Crime in urban communities, regardless of skewed statistics, havens of violence, homelessness and now the influx of illegal migrants roaming the streets, committing violent heinous crimes, and draining social service budgets. Politicians implementing laws that hamper the police and provide a free pass to criminals. But what about the cry of despair that has been simmering, festering as an open sore in underrepresented communities for decades. What happened to the black community?

Political response... empty promises and lies. It's up to the people to take immediate action to remove the political cancer from office and bring back policing by the people and for the people. If common sense policing is not returned and Americans political complacency and back-room manipulation is allowed to go unchallenged, the unacceptable status quo will remain. These communities will continue to be the scapegoats of politicians. Ignored, falling further into the void of socio- economic demise.

Chapter 4 – Stop, Question and Frisk Background

The NYPD was established in 1845 and was a force of fifty sworn officers. In 2024 the department had grown to more than thirty-five thousand sworn officers, making it the largest police department in the U.S. The department has ten divisions, six of which are devoted to law enforcement goals. The department employs an additional fourteen thousand civilians and is led by a Police Commissioner who is appointed by the Mayor of the City to serve in five-year increments.

In 1993, former federal prosecutor Rudolph Giuliani was elected mayor of New York and reelected in 1997. His platform focused on recognizing the need for a novel approach to reduce crime. That included tough strategies to reclaim the streets and restore a positive quality of life for all New York citizens.

During this pivotal time, Mayor Giuliani appointed William Bratton as police commissioner in 1999. Bratton was the former police commissioner of Boston. He had a track record of innovative police strategies. Bratton accepted the position and went to work restructuring the NYPD. Transforming it from a passive force into a department that was effective in reducing crime, promising that the department would reduce crime by ten percent during his first year as commissioner. He exceeded expectations.

The increase in the authority to address potential petty crimes and enforce *"probable suspicion"* searches led to what became commonly known as Zero Tolerance and "Stop Question and Frisk." The goal, an aggressive methodology to take guns off the street. Bratton embraced the *"broken windows"* theory. He introduced police strategies aligned with broken windows that crime should be addressed at the lowest level. The increased police presence in high crime areas and Computerized Statistical Analysis (CompStat) laid the foundation to reclaim the streets. Community-oriented police strategies instilled a renewed sense of community ownership. The focus of the strategy… to restore order and reduce the fear of crime.

Broken Windows: A Closer Look

In criminology, the broken windows theory states that visible signs of crime, anti-social behavior, and civil disorder create an urban environment that encourages further crime and disorder, including serious crimes[7]. Published in March 1982 in the *Atlantic*, the theory written by James Wilson and George Kelling suggests that policing methods that targeted minor crimes such as vandalism, loitering, public drinking, jaywalking, and fare evasion create an atmosphere of order and lawfulness. Social psychologists and police officers tend to agree that if a window in a building is broken and is left unrepaired, the rest of the windows will soon be broken. The theory was the foundation of the controversial police policy of SQF.

This theory describes the value of "attending to the previously unattended." One broken window in an abandoned neighborhood building will soon lead to more windows being inevitably broken based on the assertion that no one is tending to the building, or the street, or

---

[7] Broken Windows Theory of Policing (Wilson & Kelling) (simplypsychology.org)

the area. The results… residents of that community feel unsafe, withdraw and avoid others on the street. Physical deterioration such as trash accumulating on the streets, weeds growing up on unattended lawns, open drinking, loitering by individuals that can appear threatening. Leading to neighborhood disorder. Most communities embracing neighborhood disorder can easily be identified by gang graffiti. A mark of who controls the neighborhood, having parallel effects on the socio-economic platform of the community.

Broken windows assumes that the very presence of police officers on a "beat" will encourage the members of the community to follow the rules of the neighborhood. The *Atlantic* provided clarification: "Such as no drinking on streets, no sleeping in doorways, no teenagers loitering in designated areas, as well as efforts to fix physical damage and draw attention to strangers."

Unattended the community grabs onto the "dark side", disrespect for neighborhood rules… law breaking street crime behaviors and the breakdown of community controls creating fear and instability in the area. The simple routine presence of officers provides a sense of safety and orderliness and empowers the residents to fix things that need fixing and tend to things left unattended. Thereby establishing and maintaining stability and order.

The Initiation

Started in 1992, during the administration of Mayor David Dinkins, the first African American elected mayor of NYC. The broken window theory was tested as a new crime reduction protocol in the NYC transit system. Concentrating on the enforcement of quality-of-life crimes (low level crimes; loitering, fare jumping, spitting, etc.) and for the first-time employing stop question and frisk[8]. The results were impressive. Overall crime statistics showed that misdemeanors and felonies in the transit system was reduced by fifty-six percent in 1992.

Zero Tolerance and SQF were not a "police only" enforcement tool. At the onset, it was supported by stakeholders from across the city: minority communities, the police department, and elected officials. Desperate to reduce violent crime, they rallied around this "new" methodology of policing. Bratton was encouraged by the broken windows theory and used the theory to develop effective methods of policing. These programs included Operation Impact also known as hot spot policing. Using broken windows to continue continuity order and maintenance policing. The continuation of Mayor Dinkins 1992 "test" in the transit system was the early version of Zero Tolerance.

The enforcement resulted in astonishing numbers. More than four million probable suspicious stops were conducted between 2004 and 2012. During 2003, 160,851 stops were conducted. 506,491 during 2006. During 2008, officers documented 540,320 stops. Of that number, fifty-four percent resulted in frisks with twenty-four percent of the total number involving some type of physical force by the officer. Of the total number of stops in 2008, only six percent proceeded to the point of an arrest, and six percent of stops led to issuing a summons. And at its peak in 2011, there were more than 685,000 stops. [9]

---

[8] Factsheet: NYPD STOP AND FRISK POLICY - Bridge Initiative (georgetown.edu)

[9] https: roosevelthouse.hunter.cuny.edu/devdev/

Another study cited 4,628,936 stops resulting in 2,400,903 frisks from 2004 to 2012, while also highlighting a downward trend in stops. In 2014 there was a seventy-two percent decline. 47,000 stops were conducted, and in 2015 declining significantly to 13,604.[10] Reduction in crime achieved, order maintenance and sustainability achieved. Resources re-directed to community policing and counterterrorism.

"Broken windows" has always been a political football. Proponents professing it provided a sound foundation for the reduction of crime. Opponents stating it was a platform to allow overzealous policing and targeting in communities of color. But "broken windows" is nothing more than a theory. It is not a law enforcement practice, it's color blind. There is no race component in the Broken Windows theory. Broken Windows crosses all racial boundaries. It's an academic law enforcement theory presenting an option to mitigate crime at the lowest level. How departments implement broken windows is strictly a department decision.

Critics often point out flaws of how Broken Windows has been applied in practice. They say that broken windows encourages aggressive and harsh policing practices. Suggesting the theory is a tool that targets minorities. All rhetoric, depending on where you stand politically. One thing is certain, SQF was a success. To that point, when did it become a racial football? When politicians manipulated and meddled in policing. And when Mayor Bill de Blasio entered office in 2014, he fulfilled his campaign promise. He immediately eliminated SQF. What was the result… an explosion of crime through the end of his office in 2023. Crime in NYC's neighborhoods has skyrocketed out of control. DiBlasio can be thanked for establishing NYC as a sanctuary city, allowing thousands of undocumented and unvetted illegals to "invade the city." The invasion passed onto Mayor Adams. The city was taken over by crime and anarchy. As we turn the page, will common sense policing be allowed to return? Can SQF be reintroduced? Can it be returned to the police bag of "tools." The voice of the people will have to be the driving force. Do we remain unsafe or mitigate violent crime effectively and efficiently? It is up to you to decide.

What will alleviate violent crime? Defund the police has only exacerbated violent crime across the nation. From a historical analysis, Broken Windows theoretical policing must come off the shelf. Ironically every urban city that has defunded the police has experienced an increase in crime. It may be time to break the glass case housing the broken windows theory. It may be time to break out the old to prevent more glass being broken in the future. Because there is an emergency. Common-sense policing needs to be reinstituted. Removing political rhetoric and race politics. The facts are crystal clear. Our nation is under siege, by thugs, gangs and illegal immigrants. Crime is decimating minority communities regardless of what minority politicians are saying. Hiding behind manipulated statistics. The black community and all citizens are begging for the end of this senseless violence! It's time to return policing the streets to the police. The armchair quarterback politicians have failed to honor their responsibilities to their constituents. Enforce the laws, remove the self-serving politicians, and for God's sake, quit using constituents as political pawns.

---

[10] Stop-and-Frisk Data - NYCLU

Chapter 5 – COMPSTAT

Commissioner William Bratton introduced the Comprehensive Computer Statistics (CompStat) system when he assumed his duties as commissioner of the NYPD in 1994. He relied on the capacity of the system as a starting point to apply broken windows theoretical policing. CompStat was used to collect basic data on crime statistics, identifying criminal trends in the five boroughs of NYC and its seventy-seven precincts. Targeting specific activity and times of occurrence. The system collected timely and detailed data in a shared database, thereby creating what was initially referred to as the "weekly crime report." Which many refer to as the "hot seat." Precinct Commanders presenting their crime statistics and courses of action to the Commissioner and senior NYPD leaders. CompStat provided statistics in an unbiased racial void. It provided up to date weekly crime information. Ridding the City of the previous semi-annual report that lagged in reporting crime statistics.

CompStat was the technological innovation that was not only utilized by the NYPD. It was adopted by urban cities in the United States, Australia, Canada, United Kingdom, and Mexico. It has four core components: information-sharing, responsibility, accountability and improving effectiveness. Its benefits were identified as:

a) Data-Driven Decision Making: CompStat relies on data analysis to identify crime trends, hotspots, and patterns. Police departments can allocate resources more effectively based on this information.
b) Accountability: Regular CompStat meetings encourage accountability among police officers and supervisors. They review performance metrics, discuss strategies, and address challenges.
c) Crime Reduction: By targeting specific areas and offenses, CompStat helps reduce crime rates. Focused efforts lead to quicker responses and better prevention.
d) Transparency: Publicly sharing crime data fosters transparency and builds trust between law enforcement agencies and the community.
e) Efficiency: CompStat streamlines processes, optimizes resource allocation, and improves overall efficiency within police departments.

Remember, these benefits depend on effective implementation and ongoing commitment to data-driven practices. This is critical to the success of CompStat. As SQF reached its crescendo in 2011, field officers were becoming concerned with the effectiveness of CompStat. If CompStat was being used properly, then the reduction of crime should have reduced the numbers of aggressive UF 250 stops (NYPD form recording SQF). But in 2011, and officers in the study confirmed, UF 250's were being generated at their highest numbers since inception. Officers and police leaders realized that SQF was becoming a quota system, politically directed.

CompStat the golden goose… the senior executive analysis tool. From its inception CompStat was praised as a statistical success. But as the numbers reflected the fact that the majority of violent crime was disproportionately being committed in underrepresented communities. Opposing factions used the same data to portray SQF as a racially overzealous failure. Allegations and mudslinging garnered extensive media attention during the Guiliani – Bloomberg Administrations.

CompStat was groundbreaking. Providing a statistical analysis of the precincts with the highest rates of index crime. It allowed Commissioner Bratton and his leadership team to direct police resources. It provided an allocation tool by identifying high crime areas by category of crime. Identifying city wide crime trends, it allowed the commissioner and senior police leaders to develop a deployment strategy (SQF, auto crime units, narcotics units). The combined use of COMPSTAT generating the analysis and SQF focused the department on their strategic and operational framework. It culminated in the dramatic reduction of violent crime for over two decades. The facts are indisputable; it was an astounding evolution in law enforcement.

But CompStat as a pinpoint policing tool presented a disturbing trend in criminal statistics. It identified violent criminal activity centered around precincts in Crown Heights, Bedford Stuyvesant, Bushwick in Brooklyn, the South Bronx and East Harlem in Manhattan. The demographics of violent crimes has not changed in 2024. Since the 1990's, most violent crime continues to be committed by young black men. Regardless of being confirmed in the FBI's annual Uniformed Crime Reports (UCR). An unfortunate historical trend. SQF served as a catalyst for media coverage, exposing the plight of the black communities. Politicians ignored the communities' issues, rather, grasped onto SQF, using it as their political quota system. A quota system that became a political, not policing tool. The easiest prey… targeting minorities.

SQF became a football. The curse… politicians manipulating SQF demanding higher numbers of stops. Literally changing the goal of SQF to a political campaign slogan, manipulated to fit their race and political agendas. In the Mayoral election in 2013, SQF was a key campaign issue to court the minority vote. In fact, it was the primary mayoral campaign promise that Bill DiBlasio ran on. What happened when New York's liberal Mayor Bill de Blasio came into office in January 2014? The removal of SQF. The era of stop question and frisk came to a crashing halt. The result… violent crime in NYC skyrocketed. And in May 2020 when George Floyd was killed, every aspect of policing was attacked, the rallying cry of *Defund the Police*[11] flooded the nation. Anarchy and chaos. Not much has changed today, except not only are those same urban communities continuing to suffer urban blight, now they are being invaded by illegals, many violent criminals. The result in our urban cities… havens of poverty and violent crime.

The racial justice movement sweeping the nation. The police institution relegated as a racist enforcement tool of white America. A radical surge against the police became the national rallying cry. Protests and dramatic changes in the way the nation executed policing were under attack and still are. It was the "perfect storm" for politicians and the radical left to demand police and criminal justice system reform. Fueled through the lens of race. Criminals given more rights than law abiding citizens. The country in upheaval, politicians... instituting the

---

[11] "*Defund the police* means reallocating or redirecting funding away from the police department to other government agencies funded by the local municipality," writes University of Maryland sociologist Rashawn Ray in a June 2020 Brookings Institution blog post.

revolving door policy of "catch and release." In one door… arraigned… and out the other. Criminals free to prey on innocent citizens.

Especially urban cities. New York, Chicago, Washington D.C, New Orleans, St. Louis, Oakland, Los Angeles, Baltimore and San Francisco. Where homicides, gun violence, assaults, and carjackings have exploded since 2020. The discouraging statistics continues to reflect a surge in juvenile crime growing in one demographic across the nation… black males under eighteen. *MSN* reported that in Philadelphia, according to city data, in 2023, there were more than three thousand shootings with seventeen percent involving young people under twenty-one[12]. According to *yahoo.com.news*, juvenile crimes increased across the nation by eighty-six percent in 2023. And in 2023, NYC's John Jay College reported violent crime committed by individuals eighteen and younger rose by twenty-five percent. Adding to the anarchy… the explosion of homelessness and open borders flooding our country with unvetted illegals trafficking fentanyl, humans and God knows how many terrorists. The ability of law enforcement to curtail the influx… Zero.

And the disturbing facts have not changed; most violent crime remains black on black, in minority communities. But we needn't rely on skewed media reporting. This data has been captured in CompStat since 1994, and now CompStat 2.0.

Unfortunately, regardless of criminal trend analysis, policing has been relegated to compliance with progressive Diversity Equity and Inclusion (DEI) policy. And to meet the new DEI recruiting standards, departments, especially in NYC have lowered or eliminated physical and weight standards. Slovenly appearance, which leads to perps' ability to have the advantage (ponytails, beards, men with buns) allow the perp to easily approach from behind… in total control. Promotions in many departments are still based on race and gender.

The 2022 FBI UCR coincides with what has now become a daily occurrence reported on the evening news. The urban demographic of crime remains unchanged. That's a fact. And those cities that have eliminated SQF and aggressive police strategies, replacing them with "soft on crime" policies have one glaring fact in common. An African American government. Is there a correlation?

How can elected African Americans in positions of authority ignore the conditions in underrepresented African American communities? New York, Chicago, D.C., where funds for public programs for black citizens… more than one billion dollars, have been diverted to provide "free benefits" to illegals. District Attorney's in these now decimated cities grasped onto the new ideology of criminal justice… elimination of cash bail. At the southern border illegals immediately processed under "catch and release." CompStat that identified hot spot crime across the city, a critical resource for crime management now a thorn in the side of politicians pandering race politics. A revised CompStat 2.0 remains a statistical tool that pinpoints crime. Unfortunately, CompStat has fallen prey to politicians. Their political crystal balls, provide the "new" methodology of providing crime statistics. We'll cover the political gamesmanship used to fudge crime statistics later in the book.

---

[12] New city task force looks to address parent engagement issues, youth violence (msn.com).

Like charge cards, criminals have no fear of being caught. Going through the "new and improved criminal justice system. The revolving door. Processed, and released without consequence. Progressive district attorneys and judges favoring the rights of criminals over law abiding citizens. Releasing criminals back onto the street with reckless abandon. Many, career violent offenders and illegals. Recidivists, free to roam the streets and emboldened to continue committing crimes. Cities returned to the days of the "Wild West." More to come, as New York, and Chicago are profound examples of the disingenuous policy of sanctuary cities. With one in every five hotels in New York migrant shelters... trashed. But maybe change is not too far in the distant future.

John Lott, president of the Crime Prevention Research Center, which describes itself as a non-partisan research organization, has academic affiliations with Harvard University, the Wharton School, University of Chicago, University of Michigan and Emory University. It reported that since Alvin Bragg, the progressive New York District Attorney came into office in 2022 index crimes: Murder, Rape, Assault, Robbery, Arson, Burglary, Motor Vehicle Theft and Larceny (CompStat Index Crimes) rose twenty-six percent[13].

The NYPD police budget being cut by one billion dollars in 2012. The police stripped of officers being protected by departmental indemnification. Demonized by the city council. PolitiFact claiming NYC was once the safest city in the nation, now run by politicians who replaced public safety with race and gender politics. "Nero Fiddled while Rome Burned" is personified by the demise of the criminal justice system across the nation. And this ludicrous soft on crime policy that has decimated our nation's cities, No more than a political shell game .

Ideological rhetoric centered around racial injustice, under Mayor DeBlasio now under Mayor Adams is the pursuit to close the City Correctional facility on Rikers Island. Where the most dangerous criminals are kept pending trial. Release them to halfway houses where they will behave like ladies and gentlemen and reintegrate into society.

Leading the charge of the anti-government, social revolt, Black Lives Matter (BLM). Capturing national attention. Professing a nation of government systemic racism. Especially within the white law enforcement community. Their propaganda bamboozling politicians and underrepresented communities. Politicians, athletes and other prominent leaders jumping on the band wagon, drinking the cool aid... taking a knee in protest of systemic racism. While BLM supported the mass rioting, destruction of property, violence, all acceptable behaviors, in the name of racial justice.

But it was all a scam. BLM pocketed the contributions from underrepresented communities, extorting millions, lining their own pockets. Slinking away into the darkness. Funds promised to underserved communities squandered. Their leaders buying lavish homes... not a dime going to the improvement of the quality of life for minority communities. The consequence? Political activists, led by Al Sharpton and the likes of "squad members," Cori Bush, Ilan Omar and the vociferous Alexandria Ocasio-Cortez, have done nothing except for billowing racist rhetoric.

---

[13] *Newsweek* covers our work: "Alvin Bragg's 'Soft on Crime' Policies Face Scrutiny as Manhattan DA Goes After Trump" (crimeresearch.org)

What have they done to support their black constituents. Like Sharpton, they show up for the photo op and then disappear to their luxury homes… far away from the communities they're supposed to represent. Have they ever been to these communities, have they ever visited the police, have they ever gone on a call for service? Yet jumping on the rallying cry of *defund the police*. Leaving the police to deal with the aftermath of their hateful rhetoric. Of course, lining their pockets.

Now the political gamesmanship along racial and political lines has overridden common sense policing. The bottom line is that crime continues to surge in our urban communities. CompStat remains an obsolete dinosaur. Temporarily extinct. A viable, indispensable police tool. An effective unbiased police tool, effective in crime reduction. Eliminated because it interfered with political power struggles and agendas. Politicians using their oaths as a word salad, self-serving. While police officers display selfless service, every day placing their lives on the line. While CompStat 2.0, provided an update on criminal trend statistical analysis, it was void input by patrol officers. Rather developed by PhD's, relying on statistical data points, rather than input from the field. Especially from minority officers. Or was this another PhD level technological marvel. The equation missing its most important variable.

No surprise… the missing link… input from patrol officers. No change in 2024. CompStat certainly drove the train for senior NYPD leaders to identify strategic utilization of resources. But at what cost. What did minority officers feel about the use of CompStat, I don't think you'll be surprised. Excluding rather than including officers affected department moral and questioned their effectiveness on the streets.

Officer CompStat Quotes

"If you take a look at the same numbers, the same numbers of stops… six hundred eighty-five thousand (2011), and less than four percent actually resulted in either arrests or some types of summonses, why are we still stopping so many people.?"

"But you know, it also stems from politics. The time of the moment. The mayor wants his re-election bid."

"Creative numbering? Is it that people are not calling the police, or what? It could be a factor of things."

"It's added pressure, because when the mayor or other people get up, what's the first thing they say? "Crime is down this percent."

"Crime is down that percent. Is it? Maybe? Who knows?"

"Crime has increased since 9/11 (September 11, 2001). While we focus on 9/11, terrorism, violent crime on women, and children has increased."

"CompStat's always watered down."

"Well crime's down" – that's not good enough, "you should be stopping people." So, it's a game, and it's from higher up. "Why haven't you done as many UF 250s as last month?"

A sergeant would say "I want you to bring me five to six by the end of the week, or end of the day… whatever. I want ten movers. I want three criminal court summonses by the end of the month. It became a numbers game."

"When you take advantage of it, and you have people go out there just to get numbers… just to do that because it became a numbers game."

"That's the game, as the CO, if you go to CompStat, and if you did one hundred UF 250s last month and this month you had fifty, they'd ask "why'd you stop fifty less people?""

Statistically CompStat was effective. A standalone system, its purpose… a tool in reducing crime. It achieved what it was designed to do. Unfortunately, in 2011 and now in 2024 politicians continue manipulating the criminal rhetoric to portray how "they" have made streets safe again. But go into the underrepresented communities, talk to those citizens who live in fear. Listen to their stories of violence in the schools, drive-bys and daily shootings, just another day. How they've lost family and friends to gun violence. Statistics have no meaning or impact on the pain and anguish these people continue to endure. And as one officer made a common sense yet very prophetic statement….

"Are statistics down, maybe because the community believes that police are ineffective… why call?"

And it's not only members of the community that have expressed a reluctance on the validity of statistics. During my interviews minority officers also expressed concerns about how CompStat was applied. And I'll make a bold assumption… that their opinions remain relevant with every officer who patrols the streets in New York and other urban communities. Policing through statistical analysis as with any computer system is only as good as how the data is analyzed and applied to solve the problem. But used as a political tool, yes there was a cost. An irreparable cost. The loss of trust between the community and police.

Chapter 6 – Diversity Equality and Inclusion in Law Enforcement

Overview

Violent crime is on steroids. Social scientists and politicians created a new social experiment… Diversity, Equity, and Inclusion (DEI). DEI was the resurrection of the failed Affirmative Action program of the 1960s. Focusing not on equality, but equity. A communist balance sheet. Where total governance will be aligned with equity. But like Affirmative Action this ridiculous concept of equity eliminated the need for skills, capability, and quality. Creating a stability disaster. It has given politicians of color the opportunity to jump on the bandwagon with attempts to pad the social experiment. As with all equity systems, communism, socialism, race and gender politics, history has professed their abject failures. Driven by a democratic social agenda. Thankfully, the American people have seen the light, despite the socialist media and open political lies. We had dodged a bullet. Now will be the rebuilding. Bringing back common sense and mission focus. Especially with cabinet positions, the military, senior federal officials and our first responder community.

Has statistics and equity in policing affected crime? We'll examine what changes have been implemented to enhance and attract more minorities to join the police department. Lastly, we'll examine if inclusion of a more diverse police department has had an impact on reducing crime and providing safer communities.

Ask yourself this question… has DEI generated the desired ideological racial social justice changes? In fact, DEI has furthered the wedge in the racial divide. Urban cities, underrepresented communities remain disadvantaged. The needle of improvement has not moved. The same socio-economic problems remain unchanged since the 1960s. In fact, they are getting worse.

Politicians, *black politicians*, historically have screamed for improvements to "their" communities, Congressman John Lewis a Civil Rights trailblazer, was the Congressional Representative for the city of Baltimore for seventeen terms, yet Baltimore remains a cesspool of crime, unemployment and abject poverty. Mayor Marion Barry represented Washington D.C. from 1971 until 1991 and again from 1995 until 1999. Convicted in 1990 of using cocaine he spent six months in prison. Yet D.C. residents voted him in for another term. Because he was their savior, doing nothing for D.C. Crime was at record highs. Washington D.C. in 2024 being named by *Fox News* for the second year in a row, the most undesirable city to live in the United States. Cost of living, crime and homelessness at epidemic levels.

And now Eric Adams, the New York City Mayor has opened the cities arms to illegal migrants. Living up to the welcome slogan of the Statue of Liberty says, "Give me your tired, your poor, your huddled masses yearning to breathe free." As a sanctuary city, as is Chicago, and D.C., illegals have flooded the city. Placing a burden on the taxpayer, more than one billion dollars annually with a light on the horizon… finally. But what is the long-range damage? How our communities continue to provide a "free ride" until they are identified, granted asylum, or deported?

The migrant crisis compounded by violent criminals who have assaulted the police, gone through New York DA's revolving door, released with appearance tickets or charges dropped. The Roosevelt Hotel, a former high-class hotel, turned into a cesspool that should be condemned. Rooms destroyed, trash littering the hallways. The pungent smell of marijuana combined with the rancid smell of urine. Illegals harassing passer-by. And Alexanra Ocasio's, acting like a madame in a whore house, her district overrun with prostitutes openly soliciting and harassing residents. Supporting these illegals, law abiding sex workers.

Randalls Island the home of the FDNY training academy and NYPD Critical Response Command, once dotted by well-manicured athletic fields, became a haven for illegals. Migrant encampments and stolen vehicles dotting the shoreline. Sanitary conditions deplorable. But not to worry more are on the way. Criminals and possible terrorists among these unvetted law abiding individuals. The police are unable to turn them over to Immigration Customs Enforcement (ICE), watching as the city falls further into decay. Will the NYPD, city corrections and departments in blue states across the nation face sanctions if they choose to refuse to support ICE?

New York's residents in Bedford Stuyvesant and Harlem are battling for affordable public housing. Proponents in blue states are projecting not only the need but the desire to build more affordable housing. The result in D.C., New York, Chicago public housing- affordable housing, the infrastructure, plumbing, heat, elevators in deplorable conditions. Vermin openly roaming the complex. Violent gangs control the public spaces, unsafe for residents. Public housing is used as a recruitment center for gang members. In 2024, the economic projections for improved quality of life for minorities have gotten worse. Caught in the game of political ping pong. Nothing new, as underrepresented communities have been the forgotten class, caught for decades in the stagnant revolving door of socio-economic failure. There are too many broken windows in affordable housing.

It wasn't always that way. With the introduction of broken windows policing, Zero Tolerance and SQF, the police took back the streets and public housing. Finally providing communities a long-awaited resolve from being the victims of indiscriminate crime. A program that worked, albeit that it was tarnished with overtones of racial profiling. The question is… does the community live in fear of being victims of crime? Or do they demand action? One thing is for certain. Today regardless of what politicians present as their cover story of crime being under control… it's a lie. Crime remains out of control. Is it time to bring back Broken Windows and Stop Question and Frisk policing? Skewed statistics don't reflect the fear of decent citizens trying to survive without being assaulted walking on their way home, or their children becoming victims of senseless drive by shootings.

There can be revitalization, no doubt. When politicians quit pandering and throwing money at welfare programs. When they end crime, provide a safe environment to encourage business, safe communities to raise a family. The rest will be history repeating itself. Harlem is the prime example of a minority community that became a cultural and economic icon. The Harlem Renaissance was a cultural and economic revolution. The black community evolved into a national cultural center for almost two decades. Yet the Renaissance never received financial and political support to continue to sustain its transition. Falling into despair.

Is it time to deal with the out-of-control crime and political pandering. It is time to rejuvenate a successful police strategy. Proven in keeping our communities, especially underrepresented communities, safe. Understanding that police departments across the nation are diverse, representing the demographics of the communities they serve. Is it time to restore common sense to policing, return to the practice of "safer streets." It is time to allow citizens of all races and ethnicities and social classes the opportunity to live without fear of being shot when they step outside their home.

PolitiFact once reported NYC as "The Safest City in the Nation," now one of the five most unsafe cities in the country, joined by Baltimore, Washington D.C., Los Angeles, New Orleans, Chicago, San Francisco, and Memphis. The list goes on, capturing most urban cities in the United States. Unfortunately, there is a common denominator. One that I've mentioned previously. It can no longer be denied, ignored or covered up. Violent crime remains predominantly black on black. Remarkably black politicians ignore the facts. Bypassing the issue at news conferences, staying the course of party lines, manipulating statistics in their best interest. The safety of communities ignored. Lying to the public, making empty promises, holding town meetings, and crime prevention walks. Surrounded by their protective details. And when their photo op is done, leaving the crime infested neighborhoods. Residents returning to their homes, in the hope that they won't be the victim of a drive by shooting. Wary if they will be the next victim of needless violence. Politicians... cowards. Showing their face to remind these decent people to make sure they vote for them in the next election.

Racial Myths

Why are so many urban inner-city communities struggling with socio-economic distress and rampant crime? New York, D.C, Chicago, Oakland, St. Louis, Memphis, New Orleans are in the throes of a racial fire fueled by complacency and inaction. Ferguson, Missouri and Minneapolis, Minnesota never recovered from their racial implosions. According to *neighborhoodscout.com* these towns' crime is one hundred percent above the national average for violent crime. And these communities did not have an explosion of rampant crime because of their national exposure. They have been plagued with unconstrained violent crime for decades.

Politicians have demanded the inclusion of more black police officers as a solution to better serve minority communities. They assumed a more diverse department, racially balanced, will have a direct impact in building community-police relations. Did it? Let's look at the impact of inclusion of minority officers in police departments over the past decade.

I've done a statistical analysis... the results are startling. Urban cities that have achieved an overwhelming diverse representation of Black Mayors, Police Chiefs, City councils and police departments attaining "critical mass" have failed to achieve "safe cities." To the contrary, crime has skyrocketed... not declined. Is there a correlation? The problems go much deeper than cries to *defund the police*. They go beyond changing institutional and organizational culture and the shade of the police force.

There is a social and cultural failure, one that continues to be stimulated by ineffective policies. And political manipulation that encourages a revolving door of socio-economic decline. BLM and the current political enterprise who continues to support *defund the police* is responsible for disemboweling black youth in these cities. Their pursuit to dissolve the traditional nuclear family.[14] Another universal Marxist failure.

Only thirty-eight percent of black children under the age of eighteen live in two parent homes. More than two thirds living in a home with an unmarried black woman. Unfortunately, this research follows a continual decades long pattern. Black children living in single parent homes are seventy-nine percent more likely to end up in the criminal justice system. The second order affect, the rate of juvenile truancy. Again, apparently an acceptable norm for decades. Lack of accountability and parental supervision robs black youth the opportunity to matriculate into higher education. A domino effect. Without strong parental guidance, and solid education there is no personal responsibility. Little hope for a successful future and career.

In 2013, the Marron Institute conducted an evaluation on the racial disparity in law enforcement using a "hit analysis" model.[15] Resulting in an eye-opening conclusion. Of the African Americans stopped, one in seventeen were arrested. In other words, African American pedestrians were less likely to be arrested than whites under the same conditions. Marron's results fail to support the political perception that Stop Question and Frisk is racially biased against African Americans relative to whites.

The Hit model was objective. The analysis was performed in multiple precincts. Each having a specific demographic, and socio-economic profile. What was concluded and coincides with the FBI's Uniformed Crime Report is that communities with a large African American community and poor socio-economic stability were subject to more crimes. Communities that were more socio-economically stable, experienced less crime. SQF was not a bias tool. Officers of all races and ethnicities enforced SQF, derived from CompStat. NYPD leadership deploying officers based on statistical analysis, not demographics. Concluding that most officers that were enforcing the law were "color blind."

Racial Implications

Democratic politicians, most notably the infamous Congressional "Squad", continue to support *defunding the police*. Not only supporting *defund the police* but encouraging protestors in the summer of 2020 to riot in support of the cause. Property damage in the millions. Leading to loss of life, encouraged by socialist radicals; former Mayor Lori Lightfoot of Chicago, as well as NYC's Mayor Bill de Blasio reallocating millions to social programs. De Blasio reallocated seventy-five million dollars of the NYPD's budget to social programs. Jumping on the ideological gravy train. Seeing their opportunity to change the American enterprise from a democratic to a socialist controlled third-rate nation. The era of equity. With the exception that

---

[14] PolitiFact | Ask PolitiFact: Does Black Lives Matter aim to destroy the nuclear family?

[15] suppose hypothetically that of all the blacks and whites stopped in the Bronx, three percent were arrested, and six percent of the blacks and whites stopped in the Financial District were arrested. If we aggregated the data from the two precincts, we would mistakenly conclude that the police officers making the stops are biased against blacks, because in the aggregate sample most blacks are searched in the Bronx and have a three percent arrest rate, much lower than whites, most of which are searched in the Financial District. Thus, the hit rate test carried out without controlling for precincts would be potentially biased, or more precisely, uninformative about the racial bias exhibited by police officers within each precinct.

underrepresented communities remained excluded. Illegals being placed on the pedestal of freedom. Vice President Harris sounding the alarm of systemic racism, supporting and encouraging these national riots. Now with the radical socialist Zoran Mandani on the verge of being elected the next Mayor of NYC.

Was it effective? With violent crime skyrocketing since the killing of George Floyd, what impact did the 2020 social justice *insurrection* bring about? Nothing. Except for political pandering… moving millions from police departments to expanding *woke* policies. Promises to create more affordable housing. Pouring millions into free give away social programs… not for the underrepresented citizens… but for illegals. The plight of underserved communities remains deplorable. Unfortunately, the threat to urban communities is not the police but pandering politicians. While police hands are tied to stem the tide of vicious crime against citizens of the United States. Directed to frame their departments based on DEI race/gender platforms, eliminating physical and educational requirements. Entry level qualifications, promotions based on race. How did that go in the NYPD, let's see. Caban the police commissioner and Maddrey the black political appointed Chief of Department resigning… facing federal indictments. And more to follow.

The aftermath of these failed ideologies… police recruiting abysmal, underrepresented communities unable to receive adequate police support. Residents living in fear. What has remained consistent over the decades… politicians ignoring the social issues within the black community. Poverty, lack of education, lack of jobs. Perpetrating the circle of despair and violence, devastating young black males. The Vera Institutes, in 2012, validated that violent crime remains centered in the minority communities in NYC and cities across the nation. The facts, evidenced by the 2023 FBI UCR. Black politicians turning a deaf ear to the facts.

Why… because if they openly acknowledge there is an issue with their own race, God forbid. That would be politically embarrassing. Deflect the truth at all costs. The standard solution… spend millions to project a narrative that spins the decades old socio-economic issues. Maintain a perception of progress of their self-created problem. In other words, they use their own underrepresented communities as their pawns. Not giving a damn about these constituents, until election time. Even more prevalent with the blatant attack on the black community, by Chicago Mayor Johnson, openly attempting to reallocate millions to social programs for illegals.

The NYPD and other officials emphasized that SQF was not about *racism or racial profiling but was based solely on criminology statistics indicating that young adult, African American, and Hispanic males were statistically documented to be significantly more likely to be involved in criminal activity.*[16]

Criminal demographics the FBI UCR from 1995 to 2024 reveal the same racial pattern of criminal offenders has not changed. As a *defund the police* society, it's anticipated that the same demographic will continue to commit violent crime, at higher numbers and more violence for years to come. Driven not by the inability of the police to arrest criminals. But by politicians who look the other way, looking to achieve the black vote. Political mind sets no moral compass

---

[16] Stop-and-Frisk Procedures in NYC: How to End the NYPD's Most Racially Discriminatory Practice — Columbia Political Review (cpreview.org)

or conscience. And the political charade rolls on from year to year… decade to decade… century to century.

And blame is not limited to politicians and the police. The community also shares a segment of responsibility. I've captured one prophetic statement from a minority officer who patrolled a NYC high crime community of color. The reality… this same statement was spot on in 2003 as it is in 2024. The same urban blight remains elusive. The education system a cesspool. Minority reading and math skills in the toilet. Despair, and poverty plague these communities. Lack of parental responsibility. Many parents, especially fathers incarcerated. The streets providing more stability than in their dysfunctional homes. One of the black officers from his years working in Brooklyn's seventy-third Precinct summed up his observations from years on the job.

"Some of these communities, especially the seventy-third precinct the community culture is messed up. Openly selling drugs, violence, everyone living on welfare, having kids and the crap with no fathers keeps going. The other crap, drugs, poverty, and the other social problems I can't fix, that's politicians' fault and the people who live in the community."

From my dissertation, I identified themes related to the use of SQF. Unvarnished, no holds barred. The comments are from the study population of the officers I interviewed. They presented a unique diversity of opinions. Pro and con. All valid from their experiences enforcing SQF. What is obvious here is that there was a huge gap in communications. Patrol officers firsthand accounts never found their way up to the Commissioner. SQF strategy developed in an academic cloud. Regardless of the effectiveness of SQF, the only metric that was used to evaluate program effectiveness was CompStat. It did nothing to provide input to how officers were building community trust and developing personal relationships. These officers' interviews may not have the panache of a scholar. Not intended to. They are the verbatim comments of fine, dedicated and loyal officers of the NYPD. Similarities and contradictions. You judge.

Race – "Setting the Stage"

"Race has always been an issue. But I still think that's a person who just hates cops and doesn't want to give that cop a chance to explain himself, etc."

Biased Enforcement

"I won't say it was an issue with the powers that be. Well, you know what? Hold up. I can't speak for them. But on a street level, race did play a part, absolutely."

"Look at the numbers; you see the same. Every area has its own issues – Black or White, and that's where they got in trouble with the Federal Government."

"I'm saying that as a Black police officer. I don't know that if it was used right… don't want to be different; you want to be part of the "good old boys.""

"I mean, if I'm in a black neighborhood, I'm stopping mostly black guys. I mean that's just what it was. But I know politically, they threw a name on it, racial profiling."

"I don't think they were going after Black people; I think they were just going after people in general."

"Stop, Question and Frisk was not a race thing, for all the years on the job, it was used in high crime areas… especially in the precinct. And you know what, nothing has changed."

"No that's ridiculous, it was all based on crime, but then it became political and changed."

"Data shows that it was used in minority neighborhoods more… abusive and didn't become usage anymore; it became abusive."

Statistics alone do not present a full view of the problem. Data revealed that between 2003 and 2013, "black and Latino males between the ages of fourteen and twenty-four accounted for forty-one percent of stops." In its 2013 The Vera Institute of Justice, a progressive watch dog group in Manhattan, conducted a study titled "Coming of Age with Stop and Frisk." This research explores the experiences and perceptions of young people in NYC who have been subjected to stop-and-frisk practices. The Vera Institute, found that "forty-four percent of minority youth indicated they had been stopped repeatedly – nine times or more."17 Minorities who lived at the intersection of multiple identities, including Black and Latino, were also harmed by stop and frisk. Homeless individuals, LGBTQ communities, immigrant communities, and Muslim individuals were policed through the policy. The Director for the Center for Constitutional Rights (CCR), stated "LGBT people, young people, poor people, Arab and South Asian people and Muslims are also targets [of stop and frisk]."[18]

What is not included in these two reports is the opposite sides of the coin. Were individuals committing crimes or violations of the law at the time when suspects were stopped. Statistics reflect that the majority were stopped for zero tolerance violations; primarily for loitering, disorderly conduct, aggravated harassment, vagrancy, turn stile beating. There was no bias. The police enforcing the law with Courtesy, Professionalism and Respect. Their mission, regardless of ethnicity or race, gender or sexual orientation has not changed, enforce the law. And the law was enforced. In 2025, almost ninety percent of all violent crimes being committed in the inner city was by young black males as young as twelve… without consequence.

Regardless of what it was coined… Stop Question and Frisk, Zero Tolerance or Safe Streets. Underrepresented communities, where crime is prevalent have always displayed open hatred and negativity towards the police. That angst towards the police, not towards an officer of any specific race or ethnicity. However, black officers I interviewed stated that the community was more negative towards them. The community feeling that they had turned against their own race.

And the NYPD's enforcement of stop-and-frisk was not just used to reduce gun violence. Post-9/11 the procedure was also used as a counter-terrorism measure. Coinciding with the NYPD Muslim Surveillance and Mapping Program.[19] The surveillance program, which began

[17] stop-and-frisk-fact-sheet.pdf (vera.org)

[18] Stop and Frisk: The Human Impact | Center for Constitutional Rights (ccrjustice.org)

[19] Factsheet: The NYPD Muslim Surveillance and Mapping Program - Bridge Initiative (georgetown.edu)

under Mayor Bloomberg in 2001, monitored Muslim communities in New York and nearby states until 2014. A covert unit called the Demographics Unit. They recruited mosque informants, sent undercover officers into Muslim neighborhoods and businesses, and mapped and monitored the daily life of twenty-eight "ancestries of interest." According to a series of Pulitzer-prize winning articles by the *Associated Press* (AP), this was an unconstitutional program "never generating a lead or triggering a terrorism investigation."

What the *Associated Press* and public are unaware of, as they did not possess security clearances was information obtained from these "unconstitutional surveillances" was shared with other agencies to deter an act of terrorism domestically or abroad. The CIA, FBI, Joint Terrorist Task Forces, the National Center for Intelligence, and military Combatant Commanders. And the public will never know.

Overzealous and racially profiling… questionable. NYC and the nation were being vigilant. Pro-active to ensure another 9/11 was avoided. And in the wake of 9/11and NYC remaining number one on the terrorist attacks hit list by jihadists, the NYPD instituted policies to ensure the safety and security of "all" citizens. Authority to conduct enhanced counter-terrorism surveillance enacted through Congressional legislation. The Patriot Act.

As New York and other urban cities are exploding with illegals, flooding our cities from the southern border, sanctuary cities continue to welcome unvetted illegals. Many with criminal backgrounds, and on the terrorist watch list. Law enforcement clueless of how many criminals and terrorists are living in our communities in plain sight. Stop Question and Frisk unlawful. The importance of returning Stop Question and Frisk as an effective police "tool" more paramount for the safety and security of American citizens than ever.

Will citizens demand that law enforcement apply the law equally to illegals, or will communities continue to extend the welcome mat. Communities decimated by crime and financially depressed, while missions for social programs are provided for illegals. The police face the standard forked tongue response from politicians. Protect the citizens but accepts the results of revolving door soft on Crime prosecution. Crime without consequence. Our country can't continue down this path… is there a new day ahead?

Will More Black Cops Matter

Since Michael Brown was killed in Ferguson, Missouri on August 9, 2014, and the profound reaction of the killing of George Floyd in May 2020, political skeptics supporting the *Defund the Police* movement opened the flood gates demanding the police be defunded. Allowing and encouraging BLM activists and subversive anarchists to wreak havoc and chaos across the nation. In the wake of the George Floyd killing the ensuing riots and anarchy across the nation resulted in over two billion dollars in property damage. From NYC to Portland, Oregon. Protestors burned police stations in Minneapolis to the ground. Over eighty-seven hundred demonstrations with over two thousand officers injured. Politicians taking a knee, many encouraging the destruction. The police vilified… for attempting to maintain public safety.

What has been the aftermath of the Floyd killing? Ineffective soft on crime policies that have tied the hands of police officers, allowing criminals free reign to commit violent crimes. There has also been an outcry by minority politicians of the need to diversify police departments. Under the concept of representative bureaucracy, underrepresented communities, with more black officers would be accepted and develop better community – police trust. That a more diverse police force would affect the incidence of police involved homicides of black citizens.

Many police departments; NYC, Prince Georges County, Maryland, Washington D.C, Baltimore, Maryland, St. Louis, Missouri, New Orleans have adopted this representative equity and inclusion policing strategy. Since the restructuring of Police Departments to meet a racial DEI model what has been the effect of reduction of violent crime in the black community?[20] Have police shootings subsided, has there been a reduction in violent crime in underrepresented communities since 2020? What politicians would like you to believe is that violent crime is down. Using D.C as a benchmark, the statistics are misleading, as they are with NYC. And not surprisingly the same demographic, black youth continue to commit violent crimes.

This is based on two assumptions reported by local new stations, that have been following crime in the district (WJLA). Residents crying for police response, police unable to respond because they are understaffed. In comparison the calls for service in both D.C. and NYC are down because officers can't respond. Violent crime covered up by the inability of D.C. to police the community. And a 9-1-1 system that is a total disgrace, staffed by a group of incompetent employees… with an incentive being proposed to pay 9-1-1 operators eight hundred dollars just to show up for work. The D.C. overpaid political hack that is receiving over two hundred thirty thousand dollars a year for running a failed system. Inept negligence. Still employed. Political patronage, fitting the DEI model while black lives in the community are ignored. At least one failed 9-1-1 call directly responsible for the death of a child.[21]

Sadly, the trail of black-on-black homicides in these communities remains uncontrollable. Mayor Bowser and her DEI Police Chief have done little or nothing. Typical politicians. Under the police alignment policy of diversity and equity, violent crime in the U.S. has skyrocketed. Since the tragic death of Travon Martin in 2012, in just five hundred thirteen days, one hundred six African Americans were murdered by other African Americans. In 2023, Washington D.C. reported two hundred fifty homicides, the largest jump in twenty years. Surpassing their 2021 count, a record two hundred, twenty-seven homicides. In 2024 on track to surpass their 2023 record. Chicago and NYC trying to keep pace with their sister city.

What have D.C.'s Bowser, Chicago's Johnson, and NYC's Adams stated? Political tapdancing, irrelevant platitudes, avoiding any mention of the sporadic increase of violent crimes. What they do have in common as sanctuary cities… taking vital resources from

---

[20] Violent crime in the nation's capital is down 35% and is on track to be the lowest in 20 years, while carjackings involving firearms are down 55%, according to the U.S. Attorney for the District of Columbia.
So far this year, there have been 2,175 violent crime incidents reported compared to 3,369 for the same period in 2023, according to the Washington, D.C., Metropolitan Police Department (MPD). Over the same period, there were 4,554 violent carjackings compared to 3,002 this year.

[21] 9-1-1 dispatchers in D.C. will receive $800 bonus for showing up for all their scheduled shifts - *Washington Times*

underrepresented communities and redirecting to social welfare programs for illegal migrants. Making political speeches that neighborhoods are safe, while shots can be heard in the background. Denying that they are *defunding the police*. While police departments continue to struggle for officers, of any race, the promises of representative bureaucracy of more diverse police departments, negated by rampant crime.

What has changed… diversity policing as a smoke screen for minority legislators to push the political charge demanding criminal justice reforms. Using the race card to project their political agendas of reducing sentencing and limiting prosecution. Capitalizing on the national momentum of "*defund the police*." Far removed from their underrepresented constituents. Order maintenance policing successes of effective policing, gone up in smoke, in the cloud of public and political outcry of "*defund the police*."

Where are we… without a procedure that is effective in reducing gun violence, SQF was proven effective by proper and fair employment of officers based on hot spot policing, where there was the need. Butchered by politicians that created the stigma of SQF as a racial profiling tool. Using a justification of disproportionate stops and quotas. The facts are indisputable. And it was not enforced by "white" officers. If you wore the blue uniform, you were part of SQF enforcement. Blame easily shared across the spectrum of shareholders. No one's hands are clean.

While minority leaders posited their claims of racial bias by the police department, the reported data continued to trend criminal activity along racial boundaries. In contrast the NY ACLU relied on the NYC census to demonstrate disparate enforcement of SQF in minority communities. Minority politicians' perception, that black officers would be able to relate to the black community. That non-black officers have less interest or "buy in" to black communities. That non-black officers are more likely to use harsh police tactics. This theory is inconclusive. The media continues to report that blacks are shot at a higher percentage, by blacks in black communities, not by cops. **Table 1** below presents the truth. This national report shows that police involved shootings reflect that more white individuals are shot by the police than Black and Hispanics.

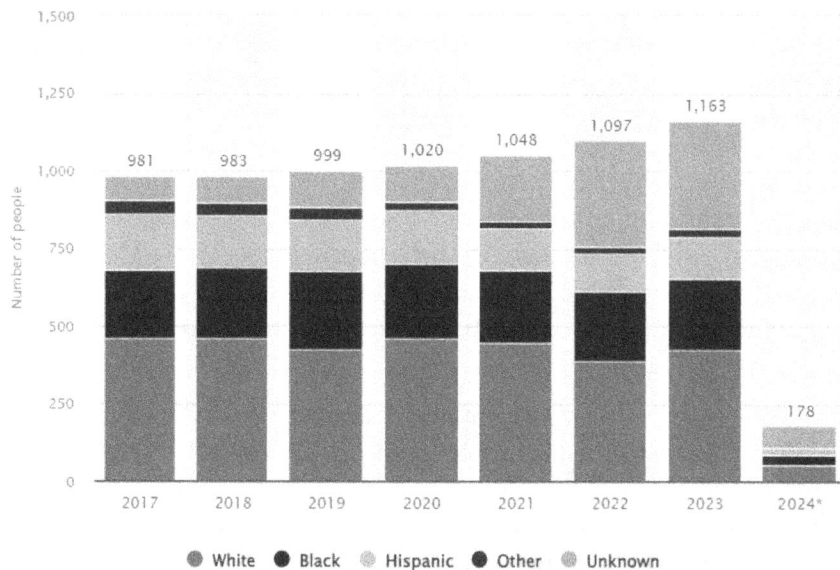

Table 1 - National Report on Police Involved Shooting

The numbers above capture the facts and dispel the media and activist perceptions that blacks are targeted by police and shot in disproportionate numbers (Statista 2024). Clearly, the most extreme narratives, in which police kill non-threatening, unarmed black men with high frequency, are false. The black share of police shootings is in line with, or even below, most measures of violent crime and criminal-justice-system involvement. Including the most extreme measures: homicides and cop-killings. Most shootings "self-initiated," by black perpetrators… officers arriving on scene responding to calls for service.

Nationally a phenomenon is occurring, and it's not good. Officers respond to calls for service most of the time, based on being dispatched by 9-1-1 operators. In the *defund the police* era, Officers are now hampered by staffing, many departments unable to respond to calls for service for nonviolent incidents. Referred to department answering machines. Officers following up on a later date. Violent and life and death calls immediately dispatched to the scene. Codified in a Department of Justice Manual, Call Management and Community Policing.[22]

Officers hamstrung. By oath they protect and serve. Now while operating in an assigned patrol sector are limited to responses. Regardless officers respond… to protect members of the community with total disregard of the racial makeup of the community. And when in need the community doesn't stop to determine if the officers responding fit the DEI police model. They want someone who is there to protect them and their family.

Are all violent crimes being reported and captured in the 9-1-1 system? Are shootings being reported as shootings? The FBI estimates that fifteen percent of shootings are misreported

---

[22] cops-w0022-pub.pdf (usdoj.gov)

under a different reporting category—mental illness, suicide by cop, officers engaged by offender. Is gun violence statistically going down in black urban communities, or are shootings being captured under another reporting category? It can conceivably be assumed that the current reduction in violent crime is mis-reported. Further based on statistical evidence in **Table 1**, there is no systemic evidence of anti-black police involved shootings. The media and politicians race baiting with irresponsible reporting. Using media propaganda to sway public opinion, forgoing the facts. Adding to the perpetuation of systemic racism.

The Crime Prevention Research Center released a study in which they addressed the following question: Do white police officers disproportionately target black people? The study noted that extremely limited data is available about the race of officers who are involved in custody deaths. Again, a unique conclusion was drawn: Black police officers are more likely to kill Black people across the board. Most important, in most cases, the race of the officer who caused the death was not known. Now in the *defund the police* era, racial statistics are required to politically demonstrate that the police are racist. Especially pursuing a conclusion that white officers are racist. All while violent crime continues to skyrocket.

The coup de grace… the clear and present danger of government and media influence to openly lie to the public. Let's view how the media uses smoke and mirrors. We'll focus on Washington D.C.

Although violent crime in 2023 was reported being down seventeen percent compared to the same time last year, crime was up significantly in 2023, especially in Ward 6, which includes Capitol Hill. The ward experienced "a one hundred, eighty-eight percent increase in homicides, a sixty-six percent increase in robberies, a forty-two percent increase in sex assaults, a fifty-seven percent increase in carjackings, and a forty-four percent increase in violent crime," according to planned testimony from Gregg Pemberton, Chairman of the D.C. Police Union, and obtained by *ABC News*.[23] Pemberton will further reveal that since 2020, the Metropolitan Police Department has lost 1,426 officers, one-third of its department. Forty percent of those leaving the department were people who resigned specifically from the police agency. He says the police force has over five hundred vacancies and notes that Police Chief Pam Smith has said it will take over a decade to fill the positions. 2024 statistics claim a reduction in crime but based on the unity of political and media collusion, I am very skeptical. Just watch the D.C. news… top stories today, violent crime, shootings.

Dispelling the myth of racial disparity, in police enforcement has been the introduction of Body Cameras. The transition to achieve transparency was intended to eliminate the racial disparity of every shooting of a minority resident being racially motivated. The "Body Cam" at first was unwelcomed by officers, but as time progressed, the body cam has resolved inconsistencies. Recording officer's actions has been instrumental in providing transparency and serving as evidence. Officers have been held accountable, prosecuted and convicted based on bodycam footage. And had served to demonstrate actions of criminals, leading to convictions. But body cam footage regardless of providing transparency, is used by the media

---

[23] Washington, DC, Police Union set to declare city crime a 'crisis' in House hearing as staffing continues to decline - ABC News (go.com)

and activist groups to twist the footage. Used as a weapon against the police in the court of public opinion. Why are the police reluctant to release body cam footage until it has been fully reviewed by investigators?

And body cams have demonstrated that police involved shootings are not racial. Body cams have shown both to be fair. That police encounters within minority communities are performed by diverse nonbiased police officers. Regardless, while body cams provide transparency, communities of color still profess police overzealous and discriminatory enforcement.

Bottom line, there is inconclusive evidence to demonstrate a major change in police departments who have expanded their racial diversity in reducing violent crime and improved community relations. The exact opposite is true. But one thing remains crystal clear. The thin blue line, regardless of the officer's race, regardless of the racial makeup of the community, serves the community they are sworn to protect. They perform their jobs in very difficult situations. Fairly and yes… color blind. It is not inclusion that has an impact in reducing crime.

The question that needs to be raised is why violent crime across our major urban cities continues to be a black-on-black phenomenon. What dynamic will it take to change cultural acceptance of violence as the method of conflict resolution? The underrepresented communities need to change their culture. They need to address violence within their own house and reverse the spiral of the crime and lost generations. Cops are not social workers, they have one job, to enforce the law. The community teaches values, morals, right and wrong. Parents, mentors are the influencers that will produce quality law abiding citizens, solid members of society. The police are a very small slice of the community. The crux of a successful community… is the community.

Members of underrepresented communities unfortunately for many, have lived in a revolving door of welfare, drugs, poverty and single parent households. Their entire life existing within a five to ten block radius. Ignored and forgotten. Black youth the most vulnerable. And when the community fails, these young men and women will find solace in the street. Graduating from the school of the streets. Majoring in violent crime. Their professors… street gangs. According to the U.S. Bureau of Labor Statistics, fifty-four percent of Black men born in the poorest households end up in the lowest earnings bracket between the ages of twenty-eight to thirty-five, compared with twenty-two percent of white men, twenty-nine percent of white women and thirty-four percent of Black women.[24] And when politicians interfere with enforcement, the opportunity through SQF and pro-active policing to capture and save a kid from falling prey to the streets, goes up in smoke. The perfect storm… communities fall further into socio-economic distress. Violent crime unchecked, and another generation of young black men and women brought into the pipeline of criminality and incarceration.

The top five police departments in the nation have been unable to curtail violent crime. Politicians supporting *Defund the Police*, demanding sweeping racial diversity. What no one sees is that over the course of the past two decades, a natural change in the racial makeup of police

---

[24] To reduce Black-on-Black crime, two criminal justice experts explain why offering monthly stipends to people at risk makes sense (theconversation.com)

departments has occurred. Listed in **Table 2** are the top [25] five largest urban departments and their current percentages of officers by race as reported by *World Atlas*.

With the outcry for equity policing, many departments created diversity, equity, and inclusion initiatives to re-frame their racial makeup. But one glaring point can't be ignored… each department that has achieved a more diverse department has seen an explosion of violent crime. Especially Washington, D.C who boasts a sixty-one percent diversity rate, yet homicides reached a thirty-year high − two hundred, fifty in 2023. And to the chagrin of the department their pursuit of a more diverse police force, has not been achieved.

The NYPD created a Deputy Commissioner position for Diversity Equity and Inclusion in their attempts to diversify the department. That intent has also failed. Chicago who created a DEI Commission for Racial Equity Action has not changed the police racial enterprise. Its mission failed in achieving crime reduction, regardless of what the politically manipulated statistics display. Chicago did attain notoriety in 2022… being named the Black-on-Black murder capital in the nation. In 2022 there was an average thirty shootings a week in Chicago, whose mayor now welcomes violent illegals.

Department	Sworn Officers	Diversity	White	Black	Hispanic	Female
New York City	36,008	53%	54%	16%**	24%	13%
Chicago	11,965	49%	47%	20%**	29%	23%
Philadelphia	6031	22%	71%	11%	11%	34%
Houston	5203	60%	37%	18%	42%	12%
Washington, D.C. Metro	3712	61%	36%	52%	9%	23%
** Department with a decrease of Black officers entering the departments in 2020 - 2022						

Table 2 - Demographics of the Five Largest Police Departments in the U.S.

Washington, D.C., the nation's capital, also forged ahead with recruiting a more diverse department. To their credit, the department achieved fifty-two percent of African American officers in 2023. Yet they used the DEI checklist to hire the current police chief. Chief Smith. Police qualifications… not important. Black female, whose claim to fame in law enforcement… DEI officer for the U.S. Park Police. What did her appointment do to reduce violent crime… nothing. But D.C. does have a Black Lives Matter mural, just four blocks from Southeast D.C., just outside an active war zone. Professing racism, it was removed when Donald Trump took office.

The NYPD eliminated several standards to "entice" minority recruits. Elimination of the one-and-a-half-mile run, waivers for certain misdemeanors. Allowing beards, ponytails and no

---

[25] The Largest Police Departments in The US - *World Atlas*

weight standards. Reflecting poorly on the department. Regardless of lowering standards, the intent has not attracted minority candidates by the droves. The same situation playing out in departments across the nation.

By lowering standards, you detract from the professionalism and reputation of the department. And this unfortunately reflects the new organizational culture of many departments. I did a deep dive and was disturbed by what I found. The applicant process in many departments may be skewed bypassing well qualified white applicants, especially legacy applicants (applicants who follow family members on the job). Using quotas, bypassing civil service hiring practices. Sacrificing quality for DEI quotas. Departments continue using an affirmative action hiring practice regardless that the Supreme Court opined that affirmative action violates the civil rights of Americans.[26]

But to the chagrin of politicians, Statista in November 2022 identified seventy-one percent of police departments across the nation remain a majority white.[27] The recruitment of Black candidates continues to be difficult to achieve. A review of the NYPD and Chicago PD between 2021 and 2023 reflected a three percent reduction in the numbers of Black officers.

Every city identified in **Table 2** are overrun by crime. Politically controlled by a black mayor and city council. African American Mayors: Bowser in D.C., Adams in New York, Johnson in Chicago, Parker in Philadelphia. Whitmer, Mayor of Houston, Texas, is the only non-minority. But each city pushing an effort to recruit minority candidates. The sixty-four-thousand-dollar question… will a predominantly minority police department reverse the downward spiral in any of these cities that have been plagued by crime for decades? Politicians certainly bamboozled the public… that equity policing would solve their cities out of control violent crime.

Mayors of ravaged minority communities hold meetings, do crime walks (with their protective details), and promise to alleviate crime. Promises that are never kept. Then they go back to their protected cocoons, far removed from citizens residing in literal war zones. In D.C., Mayor Bowser and her minion Chief Smith have done at least two crime walks in the past six months (2024) in Southeast D.C. Then almost like clockwork you can watch the evening news. Another shooting… another life has been lost in southeast. In St. Louis, politicians refuse to walk the streets day or night… it's too dangerous. And in NYC, Mayor Adams shows up at crime scenes, surrounded by his protective detail. When done, he runs back to the protective walls of Gracy Mansion.

What should be mandated is that all elected officials, as a condition of employment live in these distressed communities. Experience the fear and anguish. Be forced to live there until they figure how to apply "equity" to protect all citizens… *without a protective detail*. Be the servant of the people, not the people the servant of pandering politicians.

Political rhetoric aside, there is only one effective solution… common sense, aggressive policing. And it needs to be re-instituted immediately. The current prospect of soft on crime

---

[26] Supreme Court strikes down affirmative action programs in college admissions - SCOTUSblog
[27] Police officers by ethnicity, U.S. 2020 | Statista

"coddling" has exacerbated not reduced violent crime. Totally ineffective. The theory of *Representative Bureaucracy*, in this case the police department, represented by the racial makeup of the community, will provide for their well-being has been tried and failed. You need quality, dedicated, intelligent, physically fit, officers capable of applying the law fairly and effectively.

The intent of the Violence Interrupters program in D.C. and NYC is to provide mentors who can mitigate violent crime. Mostly former convicted felons… now under a new mayoral *woke* proper pronoun… returning citizens. Freedom of information requests to the D.C. agency who runs the program, Office of Neighborhood Safety and Engagement (ONSE) were blindly continuing to spend thousands based on payroll/performance documents that were several months old. Let's not forget who was supposed to be benefiting from this mismanaged program.

What was not available were employee "sign in" documents, performance and evaluation plans. Apparently ONSE was negligent in monitoring contract performance. These companies and their returning citizens should be prosecuted and return to being convicted felons. Yet D.C. funds the program.

Where did the money go? Accountability atrocious. It was discovered that a city council member was taking bribes from the five minority companies to manipulate the D.C. violence interrupter contracts. And when reporters went to contact these companies, their offices were vacant, fraudulent fronts.[28] No one from the Mayor's office or anyone in the Office of Neighborhood Safety and Engagement (ONSE) could provide answers. Their response in June 2022 – "the data are too scattered and incomplete to pinpoint the program's impact on violent crime.".

And now Bowser and her Public Safety Commissioner Appiah unable to justify the program. However, it would be a plausible assumption that as the police department is incapable of making significant reductions in violent crime… the violence interrupter program has been a total failure and had no impact in the minority community. But every violence interrupter fits the bill of the DEI criteria.

And in NYC, the Cure Violence program has reported that violent crime has been reduced in 2022 and 2023 respectively. Yet the Office of Neighborhood and Public Safety have no data demonstrating what metrics identified the success of its Violence Interrupters. One single metric is being used… numbers of guns taken off the streets by officers. Not on the reduction of violent crime in minority communities.

Without quantitative statistics, the assumption must be made that cities are negligently paying for programs that failed to meet their intent. No more than political pet projects. An effort to justify a pipe dream that convicted felons, whose only experience is committing crime, can provide counseling and mentor at risk youth. Not trained successful role models. Another farce and failure of municipalities that embraced the *defund the police* movement.

---

[28] DC's violence interrupters may not be helping to curb rising crime, audit says - WTOP News

Chapter 7 – Comparative Analysis

New York City's Commissioner Bratton was a leader in community outreach in his attempts to actively recruit minority officers. Fully supporting the increase of police recruits representing a more diverse department. In 2015 he stated his assessment of the problems in NYPD's attempts to recruit black officers, after a year of minority outreach. There are no surprises and reflects a nationwide problem. He is quoted:

> *"Attempts to represent the minority demographics of NYC within the NYPD remains a significant challenge. Candidates within the minority communities of the five boroughs of New York Cities are nominal at best. Lack of education, prior criminal records, disciplinary problems, poor physical condition, deny young minority men and women the opportunity to join the ranks of the NYPD. Regardless of the NYPD's efforts through the NYPD Cadet program, various mentorship programs provided through precinct Community Affairs units, the pool of candidates remains culturally hindered. With the educational requirement to join the NYPD changed from a high school diploma to an associate degree, the gap of eligible minority candidates has increased.".*

Bratton was spot on. You need a highly professional department, and lowering standards to achieve a political goal, is not the solution. Yet that's exactly what the NYPD adopted.

NYC is not the only police department attempting to make strides in diversity, many have already achieved a more representative department. The effect… that as departments have diversified, crime has also risen significantly. There is a buy off with *defund the police* and the pursuit of DEI. Do we sacrifice quality and ability for political ideologies and public safety?

Assessment of Metropolitan Police Department (MPS) (Washington, D.C.) Minority Staffing

1. **Historical Context**:

   In the late 1990s, MPD was sixty-seven percent Black. Led by then-Mayor Marion Barry. These policies aimed to address racial disparities and increase minority representation.

   In this decade over half of the minority officers who entered the department during this minority surge, reached retirement age. Replacements were less likely to be black or native to D.C. Negative perceptions and lack of support in the era of *defund the police*. The educational requirement for recruits to have two years of college, and most disturbing… the lack of political support, more concerned with race than public safety.

2. **Current Situation**:

   Currently MPD still has a ratio of 55% minority officers. But the trend in MPD annual reports over the course of the past three years continues to reflect reduction in minority officers.

   The complexion of MPD is heading in a reverse direction. Slowly returning to a department that will return to the majority… Caucasian officers. Does the department pursue a DEI recruitment platform or do they execute recruitment to bring on candidates who want to be police officers, are willing and able to execute the job.

3. **National Trends**:

Other large cities across the U.S. have actively worked to hire and pursue a DEI recruiting platform. Several have achieved their goal; NYC, Los Angeles, Chicago, St. Louis and Baltimore have seen an increase in minority police presence.

According to a U.S. Bureau of Justice Statistics report, minority police representation doubled from 1987 to 2013, reaching twenty-seven percent nationwide through a normal cycle of changes in jurisdiction demograhics.

4. **Arrest Disparities**:.

Despite these efforts, crime in D.C. remains disproportionate. From 2013 to 2017 D.C.'s population was forty-seven black. Of that, racial demographic accounted for eighty-six percent of arrests. In 2023, blacks represented seventy-two percent of arrests.[29]

Despite some progress, neighboring jurisdictions, Montgomery and Arlington Counties also face similar challenges. Montgomery County's police force remains eighty percent white, while Arlington's has held steady at more than sixty percent white for at least five years. But for all the effort and political pressure to diversify the police, what is the overall goal? To affect racial equity, or to maintain an effective diverse police department.

Is it to have a blended department for show and tell or is it to have well trained dedicated qualified officers enforcing the law? Is it to rally behind affirmative action and DEI quotas? Will more diverse departments influence arrests of minority offenders? Especially where the efforts to diversify departments encompass communities which have been high crime areas for decades. Will "racial profiling" be justified… or redefined? Over eighty-five percent of violent crimes committed by black male perpetrators. Yet Alvin Bragg, the NYC DA has implemented policies that allow violent offenders right back in the community, within hours. When black officers' arrests are mainly black and Latino are they categorized as racists? Are they racial profiling? Are the police targeting blacks indiscriminately? Is it racial profiling or is it identifying high crime areas, where the perpetrators reside in a minority community?

If a black officer shoots a black suspect, is it systemic racism? Is a black officer expected to enforce the state penal code differently when dealing with a dangerous black suspect. All officers attend the police academy; all officers must complete the POST (Police Officer Standardized Training) and any required state mandated courses. All officers are trained in the continuum of deadly physical force. And there have been changes in policing. Not because of racial inequities but because procedures were not effective and did not protect the public. Especially no-knock warrants. Warrants intended to provide a level of surprise when executing a warrant to apprehend a violent perpetrator. Too many times, leading to the death of an innocent individual.

Most notably, Breonna Taylor, age twenty-six, March 13, 2020[30] who was shot and killed in Louisville, Kentucky. Officers executing a no-knock warrant to arrest her boyfriend on drug

---

[29] 2020_06_15_aclu_stops_report_final.pdf (acludc.org)
[30] Police shootings: What happened after controversial cases | CNN

33

charges. No warning, surprise achieved, Taylors boyfriend, a convicted felon, firing at police with a handgun. Shots exchanged, and Taylor caught in the crossfire and killed. The outcry of Taylors death led to changes in police use of no-knock warrants nationwide. No knock warrants eliminated in most departments. A dangerous use of force changed where officers must announce their presence before breaching a residence. Why, because of the voice of the people in underrepresented communities.

No officer, regardless of race or ethnicity goes on patrol with the intent to shoot someone. Officers go into every community to serve and protect. Officers are trained in cultural awareness, ethics, and diversity, at the academy and continued during in-service training. On the street patrol officers go from their formal academy training to the street. And on the street, they are thrust into a new form of law enforcement… the "law of the street." And in many underrepresented communities, street law doesn't project systematic racism, but inherent mistrust and hatred for the thin blue line.

Regardless of race and ethnicity of officers, communities remain apprehensive. Refusing to cooperate in criminal investigations. Nothing new, the law of the streets provides a blanket, criminals are allowed to hide in plain sight. Even if they know the perpetrator and the heinous crime that has been committed. "Street law" … mistrust, and fear of reprisals, the number one critical factor why crimes remain unsolved in underrepresented communities.

The double-edged pendulum swings both ways. What is clear is that the old paradigms of black and white police discrimination are past police history. As departments continue to diversify, the paradigm of police being systemically racist is no longer a viable argument. Officers perform one job, enforcing the law. In the twenty-first century shifting demographics of police forces will remain a complex issue. However, the argument of black males being inadvertently shot by police officers as a sporting event in the game of systematic racism, is absurd. Checks and balances are in place to ensure transparency.

And police recruiting will always have a metric of hills and valleys. The hills and valleys dependent on who desires to become a police officer. The variables: gender, race and ethnicity will fluctuate as the country's demographics fluctuate. As it has in the NYPD, it will occur naturally as the city's demographics change. The single most important issue that seems to be left out of the diversity equation… becoming a police officer is a personal choice. It's the desire to live by rules, maintain standards, and enforce the law for all citizens. And that can't be accomplished by DEI quotas. The debate will continue, and policing will remain a hotly contested political football. Played out by babbling political buffoons for years to come.

Chapter 8 – Ferguson Effect

In 2014, Michael Brown, was shot and killed by a Ferguson, Missouri Police Officer. The facts of the case after a lengthy trial confirmed that Brown was attempting to wrestle the officer's weapon from his holster. The officer was in fear for his life, a struggle ensured, and Brown was fatally shot. The aftermath of a white police officer shooting an unarmed black teenager triggered national outcry. Black communities erupted in cries of police brutality and police racism. White officers branded as racists, systemic racism, racial profiling a standard police practice, open discrimination in the black community.[31] After days of riots, residents, mainly African American, looted and destroyed their community in protest. President Obama sent his Attorney General Eric Holder to Ferguson to "apologize" to the black community for the racist police. It also led to President Obama's White House-driven initiative for police reform, Task Force on Twenty-first Century Policing,[32] the results like many of the Ferguson recommendations curtailed, placed on the shelf, why… community mistrust.

In many departments across the nation, including Ferguson, the Department of Justice (DOJ) mandated actions to better diversify the police representing community demographics. In Ferguson, the DOJ retained oversight of these mandated changes to the police department. Meant to appease or have the perception of appeasing the disparate racially biased police department. It practically eliminated traffic stops of minority members of the community and directed expungement of unpaid fines. Did that help, detract, or maintain the status quo of traffic violations?

The results of the DOJ mandates in Ferguson were heard around the world. The national outcry that all police were inherently racist, demanding police reform. Ferguson was the opening salvo for dynamic changes in community policing. And Ferguson complied. Where is Ferguson today? Today, Ferguson's crime rate is one hundred, six percent above the national average. Violent crime remains above national levels at one hundred, seventeen percent The poverty rate is twenty-one percent, and the demographics remains predominantly African American (seventy-one percent). The socio-economic condition has not changed, and the percentage of Black police officers is six percent. The DOJ mandates having achieved no measurable return. Where was the enhancement of a more fair and equitable enforcement? How did the community rally to support the change? Never a one-way street, the road to successful communities are a three-lane highway; political, community, police, and when one of those lanes is closed, the triad of community change cannot move forward.

---

[31] Timeline of events in shooting of Michael Brown in Ferguson | AP News

[32] In December 2014, President Barack Obama appointed a task force on 21st century policing charged with identifying best practices and offering recommendations on how policing practices can promote effective crime reduction while building public trust. To inform its work, the task force facilitated seven listening sessions, hearing testimony from 140 witnesses and reviewing volumes of written testimony and submitted its final report to the President in May 2015. This implementation guide is a companion to the task force report. It is a tool that provides guidance on implementing the task force's 59 recommendations and 92 action items and serves as a resource for law enforcement, local government, community members, and other stakeholders interested in concrete examples of ways to turn the task force recommendations into action.

Historically since Michael Brown's shooting, the community has remained plagued by crime committed by its residents. Ferguson now a forgotten memory. The community has done little or nothing to change their socio-economic condition. Local politicians have all rolled up their magic carpets and given up. Returning to other media events to pander to the public to remain in office. But Ferguson has made improvements to diversity. They have a Black Mayor and Black Police Chief. As does NYC, Baltimore, D.C., Chicago, and their next-door neighbor St. Louis. And Ferguson has followed suit with their sister cities. Crime, poverty, unemployment has not changed for the better. It's gotten worse. Ferguson proved from the onset that "Soft on Crime" doesn't work, factually or ideologically.

The reverberations and scrutiny emanating from Ferguson against law enforcement was the spark that started the *Defund the Police* era. Leading to intense public negativity towards police officers, regardless of race. Creating a new police theory, one that has changed the reluctance of officers to engage in proactive policing.

The "Ferguson Effect," was coined after police observed a surge in violence following the 2014 shooting of Michael Brown in Ferguson, Missouri. With the perception of institutional racism fueled by the Obama Administration. The negativity towards the police trickled down to the state and local levels. Officers on the firing line. Every arrest, every public interaction scrutinized by the media, especially white officers. The scapegoats of minority politicians and activists like Al Sharpton.

The police held accountable for failed policies, attacked as systemically racist. Lack of support from political administrations at the state and local levels. With local policies amended, removing liability for police misconduct on the department. Officers facing civil liability and financial ruin, bearing the burden for lawsuits of police misconduct. Officers retreating, reluctant to be proactive. Hesitant to enforce the law. And where has that led us in the past three years, during the Biden – Harris administration? Criminals empowered to commit violent crimes at record numbers… without consequence. Politicians… the real enemy. The second order affect… Arrests went down, crime went up. The scales of justice favoring criminals. Crime statistics showing record lows in violent crime. The reality, officers no longer proactive, not making arrests. Law enforcement by smoke and mirrors, manipulated by politicians. Realizing that officers may or may not respond to a call for a violent crime in progress. And *no cash bail* placing criminals back on the street.

Since 2020, the political climate has allowed the criminal enterprises to control urban areas. Who has borne the result of *soft on crime* law enforcement? The same communities that have borne the brunt of political malfeasance for decades. The underserved black communities. The communities that were supposed to benefit from changes in the new era of *woke* enforcement. What's worse is that its black politicians have been the cause of the scourge of crime in the black communities. The game of pandering, and manipulation. Keeping these communities in fear, holding them hostage… tying the hands of the police… for votes.

The urban footprint since 2020 has changed dramatically, especially with the explosion of illegal immigrants. Surging across the border, bringing to this country, their cultures, diversity… gang affiliations, poverty and criminal activity. No desire to assimilate, bringing in communicable diseases that had been eradicated in this country (polio and measles). Strangling the resources (housing, welfare, social services and medical) of this country. Needy American citizens benefits taken away to support the migrant surge. Finally in 2025 the Trump Administration aggressively enforced immigration law. Law enforcement was allowed to protect the citizens of "this" country.

Public administrators, community activists and the community itself need to lead the charge to find the solutions to reverse what has become a socio-economic underclass. Is it cultural design of those who live in those communities? Is it the inability to assimilate? What prevents upward mobility and stagnation in these communities? Surely not political lies or false promises.

Ethnic communities, need to come together. Just as the immigrants did at the turn of the century. They need to unify, not live in a salad bowl.[33] With urban communities' home to multiple ethnicities, their communities remain segregated by race. Co-existing, but not united. This view expresses the ideology of multiculturalism, which goes far beyond the demand that ethnic differences be acknowledged rather than disparaged. Immigrants who came to this country at the turn of the century arrived with the intent to assimilate. Unify under one banner and adopt the American culture. They came to become Americans. Ghettos morphed and advanced in social and economic standing. Ghettos were well established by European Immigrants; the Italians, Germans, Russians, Jews, all lived in squalor, with no public assistance. Communities refused to accept the status quo. They had lofty expectations, and the family was the driving force. Responsible and accountable. That is not the case today.

Communities are divided. Reliant on their ethnic slice of the urban community. Community engagement "holding the members of the community accountable" nonexistent. The difference between immigration at the turn of the twentieth century and now, communities assumed responsibility for the framework of their communities. And respect was inclusive of the community. A child misbehaving would be disciplined by another adult of the community, without question. Today if that were to happen, there would be a confrontation, lawsuit, or possible physical altercation. The bottom line… if the community fails to contribute, if they refuse to assume responsibility for the framework of their communities, every aspect of sociological stability and improvement will be in vain.

It takes a tribe. And there is no tribe. Only a salad bowl. Statistics are resoundingly clear; without resolution, age eligible minorities will continue to remain ineligible to become police officers and continue to struggle to become successful. Facing a life of adversity, to include criminal activity. The fault… politicians, who refuse to address the root cause of community socio-economic conditions.

Meeting departmental diversity is not a failure in police organizational culture. It's a failure of the political representation that failed underrepresented communities for decades. Even the ACLU, the champion of the underrepresented have voiced their concerns of equity quotas as crime surges out of control. Claims that the NYPD has an internal organizational culture of racial bias… unsubstantiated. The fact is the NYPD is the most racially diverse department in

---

[33] Melting Pots and Salad Bowls | Hoover Institution Melting Pots and Salad Bowls

the nation. Fifty-two percent of the NYPD are from races other than white. What must be crystal clear, is that creating more diverse departments is not all about "black and white.".

SQF still exists. But on a much lower enforcement scale. In 2011 at the height of SQF over six hundred eighty-five thousand people were stopped. In 2023 a relatively small segment of NYC residents was stopped, only sixteen thousand. But what has not changed... the same precincts... in minority (Black and Hispanic) communities remain plagued with crime (40, 41 (Bronx – Hispanic), (73, 75 (Brooklyn – Black). Those are facts, no bias, or political influence.

In 2011 fifty-three percent of stops in NYC were on black residents. The percentage of stops in 2023 remained relatively the same, fifty-nine percent. And the NYPD continues to diversify. With a more diverse police force aligning to the community, the prospect of a "white" officer stopping someone has dropped by more than thirty percent. Relevance to the contrary that SQF targets minorities.

But minority communities continue to believe that a disproportionate number of stops and frisks intentionally target Black citizens. Fueled by activists, who live far from underrepresented communities. Minority communities mistrust the police. Throughout the "SQF Era" community activism swelled and demands for reforms and changes to police tactics rallied politicians. The same war cry that drove Defund the Police. Urban politicians succeeding with one outcome – a recidivist open house, and urban shooting galleries. Race politics at the expense of innocent citizens.

In 2024 these same clueless politicians are attempting to reverse the chaos and anarchy that they created. Attempting to pass restrictive gun legislation to reverse the violence. Criminals normally don't abide by legislation, only the law of the street. Flawed...

1. Criminals do not care about what's written on a piece of paper.
2. Active policing is taboo.
3. Policing based on "equity," not taking criminals off the street.
4. Skilled experienced cops, predominantly white, leaving in droves. Retiring or driven out by politicians' hell-bent on re-aligning police departments under a DEI platform.
5. The mass exodus of officers leaves a huge gap in providing recruits with Field Training Officers to teach them to be effective "street cops.".
6. The inability of Urban departments to recruit minority officers.
7. The Ferguson Effect.
8. Being vilified across the spectrum of political and community agitators.
9. And most important... criminals are strategically more organized than the police, able to "hide in plain sight.".

And now in New York City, a new term is on the horizon... the "Penny Effect." Daniel Penny a twenty-five-year-old former Marine, encountered what police describe as an emotionally disturbed person. Jordan Neely, age thirty, with a history of mental illness, drug abuse and forty-two previous arrests. On May 1, 2023, Penny was riding the subway when Neely burst into the subway car, ranting, and making threats that he was going to kill passengers and didn't care if he was killed. The passengers feared for their lives. Penny did what Marines do, he jumped into action to save lives. He quickly gained control of Neely, wrestling him to the ground, placing his arm around his neck. To restrain and prevent Neely from following through with his threats. Several other citizens, who happened to be minorities, jumped in to assist restraining Neely. All caught on camera. When the police arrived, Neely was conscious. He was taken to Bellevue Hospital where he died. The police questioned Penny, who cooperated… no charges were filed. It was determined that Penny violated no laws and was released. His actions… saved lives.

Until Alvin Bragg decided to prosecute, determining that the evidence demonstrated that Penny had killed Neely. That his actions, placing his arm around Neely's neck, were the direct cause of Neely's death. Regardless that the autopsy proved that Neely had drugs in his system that may have also contributed to his death. The real reason was that Neely was black, and Penny was white. Penny intervened because he was a racist. The facts… Penny jumped in when he saw fellow citizens threatened by a psychotic out of control. Making threats to kill passengers. Neely was out of control… a public safety threat. Cut and dry. But Bragg and the prosecutor used the race card. In May 2023 Penny was indicted for involuntary manslaughter and assault in the first degree. For a year and a half, the DA and the Court pursued Penny, painting Neely as a victim.

Eventually after a year and a half of testimony, the case was sent to trial. When the jury was unable to unanimously agree on a verdict to the charge of manslaughter, the judge attempted to bully them to go back and continue deliberations. Imposing an Allen charge. This refers to jury instructions given to a hung jury urging them to agree on a verdict. They have a controversial history, with critics warning they can intimidate jurors to change their verdict.

The prosecutor, to gain a victory on the count of criminally negligent homicide, dropped the manslaughter charge. Attempting to play legal games, dangling the carrot, and see if the jury would convict on the lesser count of aggravated assault. Thankfully, the jury refused to be intimidated. Bragg, his prosecutors, and the judge all colluding to attain a conviction. Black Lives Matter coming out of the woodwork joining Bragg and his legal thugs in their racist rants.

But justice for Penny was served. In December 2024 he was acquitted on all charges. Vindicated, temporarily, now facing a wrongful death suit by Neely's family. Penny's trial another DEI farce. But there was irreparable damage done to citizens across the country, damage that was to see a tragic ending to a defenseless woman.

New Yorkers for the most part mind their business, but like Penny, when a life and death situation can't be avoided, they like all decent people, will come to a victim's aid. We did it on 9/11, when New Yorkers displayed immeasurable courage helping save lives. We do it daily… when we help a senior citizen who has just fallen. We give a homeless person a couple of bucks. We give up our seats on public transportation. New York is full of acts of kindness, of helping others in desperate conditions. And while pandering politicians play the race card, the acts of kindness are performed regardless of race. New Yorkers' kindness extends way past the color of one's skin or the language they speak.

But the prosecution of Daniel Penny rang out throughout the city. It did irreparable harm. Good decent people who once would have intervened to save a life, now sitting on pins and needles. Apprehensive to step forward and help. Especially if you're not the right race. In fear that you will be the next good Samaritan who will have to endure being charged with a crime, dragged through the court of public opinion. Having to be in the spotlight, your reputation tarnished. Dragged through the court system, eviscerated, and forced into financial ruin. Is it worth it?

And the "Penny Effect" coming to the forefront less than a month after he was acquitted. A stain on the City, a stain on those who's soft on crime policies are in the opinion of this author a direct cause of this tragedy.

On December 23, in the Coney Island subway station, an illegal animal saw a woman sleeping in a subway car. He approached her, and without hesitation, intentionally doused her with lighter fluid and lit her on fire. He then sat across from her watching her be burned to death!! The subway car was full of commuters. NOT ONE PERSON CAME TO HER AID!! She died a horrible needless death. The savage was arrested and charged with first degree murder. This tragedy could have been avoided, but for the intervention of passengers. They sat frozen in fear, unwilling to come to the aid of another human being.

Why did she die without anyone's aid… rumblings from reliable sources, that the passengers were afraid that if they helped, they may face prosecution. That the DA, with their history of providing illegals and violent offenders with more rights than citizens could possibly face scrutiny and possible prosecution if they would have intervened. Had they physically intervened in restraining or using physical force to deter this illegal savage, they would be identified as racist, their lives ruined. The Penny Effect. Why bother to help a fellow citizen, at what cost? Criminals are protected, while the decent citizen is crucified. The new mantra… every citizen for themselves. Decency and stepping forward a taboo… a kiss of death. All founded on DEI, race politics, and personal and political agenda. Lives, all lives inconsequential.

The Ferguson effect changed policing from a pro-active to reactive profession. Now the Penny Effect is the new mantra for the civilian community. When you see your fellow citizens in a life-threatening situation, when you can make the difference… do nothing. I pray that as our nation transitions, common sense, fairness and not being afraid to help our fellow citizens becomes the shining light of this country.

Chapter 9 – A Double-Edged Sword

Throughout the life cycle of SQF, a policy assessment to evaluate program effectiveness has never been performed by NYC. Unchallenged, the numbers rose to staggering levels… more than six hundred, thousand in 2011 (**Table 3**). SQF became embroiled in a political battle. Polarized along racial lines. Politicians riding the wave of crime reduction, accepting complacency… all while index crimes continued to drop.

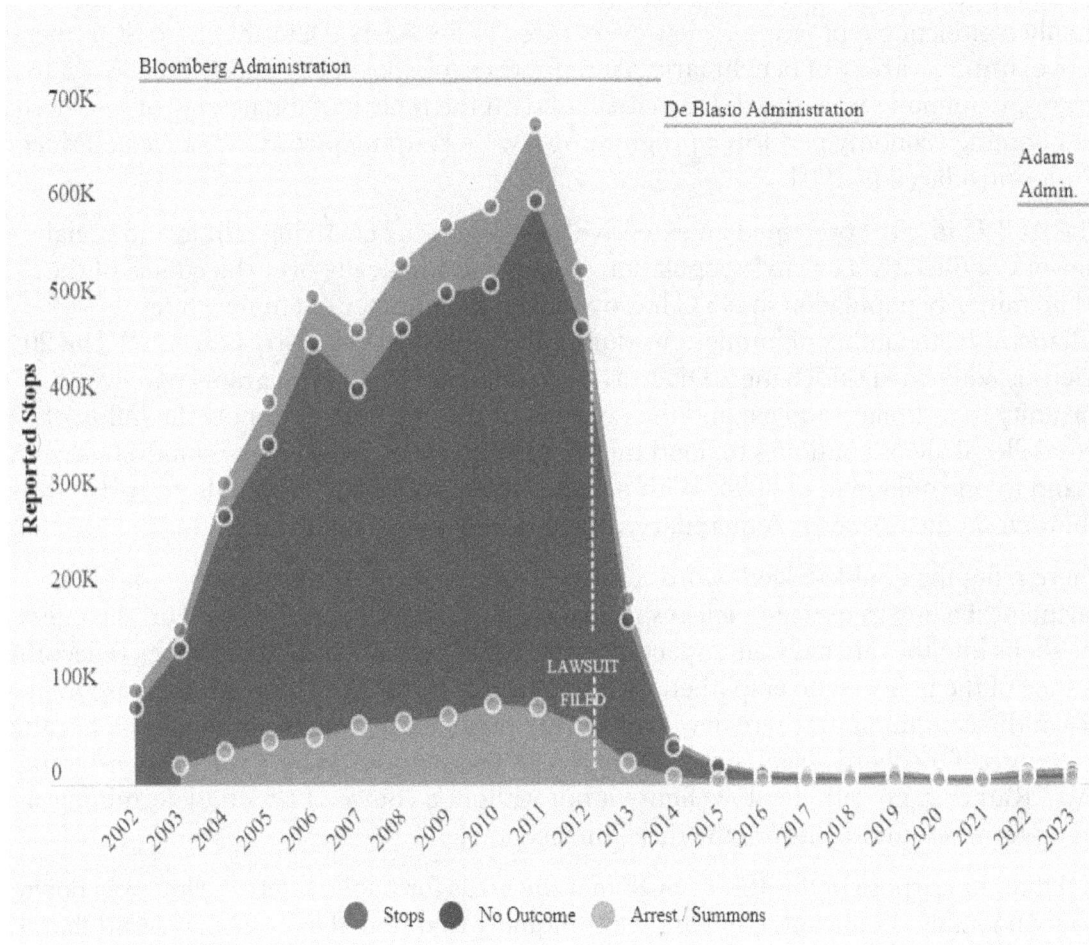

Table 3 - Stop Question and Frisk Over Time

Initially SQF numbers reflected officer's discretionary searches based on probable suspicion. Was it an effective tool to reduce index crimes.? Did it work… absolutely. The framers of SQF accomplished a dramatic shift in crime reduction. A restoration of the vitality of the city, surging economy, NYC the global tourist melting pot. Mass transit was solvent and safe. New

Yorkers not only felt safe, but with the confidence that the police protected them. The NYPD... the premier law enforcement agency in the world.

The cold hard truth... the City Administration became totally reliant on SQF as their go to tool to fight crime. The question... once the city achieved and sustained the acceptable levels in crime reduction... was an elevated level of aggressive policing still necessary? Where was the venue to perform the standard Public Administrative Policy Review? As a doctor in Public Administration from the policy perspective, public administrators work for the people. They are the stewards of effective policy and public funds. In plain language, the government is supposed to be mindful of the effectiveness of programs. To ensure their veracity and effectiveness. Normally conducting a program review every three to five years. Determining if SQF met its objective, using a variety of benchmarks. And if successful, looking to redistribute assets to other programs. Common sense. But did the city, based on the rebirth of the heyday of safe streets, and a booming economy perform a program review? A startling picture was revealed since SQF was introduced in 1994.

The ACLU in 2010 presented an extensive analysis on the changing ethnic and racial framework of the city. The city's population changed dramatically over the course of the SQF era. The minority population in NYC has overtaken the number of ethnic whites. Simultaneously, the influx of immigrants during the 1990s rose by thirty percent.[34] The 2017 US Census confirmed this change. Diversity was welcome. Legal immigrants had every opportunity to assimilate and expand the diversity of the city. However now the influx of unvetted illegal aliens continues to flood the city. Estimates of between one hundred seventy thousand to one million as of 2024. With no clue which are violent criminals, terrorists, or here as a burden on the taxpayer. A quandary... who is to blame... politicians.

Therein lies the double-edged sword. First, at fault, the City Administration, and Police Department. Failing to execute their respective public policy responsibilities. Did the influx of illegal aliens into the city have an impact on crime? Did cultural and ethnic issues reflect the ignorance of the police to be empathetic to these new arrivals? Was there an increase in index crimes in the communities where new arrivals (the political rhetoric to eliminate the negative connotations of the word illegal) reside? Where was the analysis? Where were the program reviews? Rather... go with the flow, figure it out without a course of action, determining short- and long-term resources, just roll the dice. Unacceptable.

SQF had its purpose in the 1990s. SQF met the goals for public safety. Crime was down, economy booming. Politicians enjoying the tranquility that settled over the city. And that was the acceptable norm for two decades, under the guise of... if it's not broken... it doesn't need to be fixed. But with any city, there are fluctuations, highs and lows, the tides of socio-economic and public safety conditions will change. It is a natural course of the lifeblood of the city. Program evaluations are not performed... "just because." They are performed to ensure the best interests of the public. With SQF, the city didn't even take the Hoover out of the closet!

---

[34] https://www.nyclu.org/data/stop-and-frisk-data

What no one was prepared for was the social revolution of equity and inclusion following the death of George Floyd. Overnight the country exploded with outcries of racial injustice. Anarchists destroyed property; several individuals were killed in the ensuing protests. Where was the balance… there was none. Chaos and anarchy enveloped the nation. Politicians surrendered to the "will of the people." Taking a knee… all for political positioning. They sold their souls disregarding hard working constituents, abandoning them for radicals. As this new era descended on our nation, the brunt of this tragedy is evident in underrepresented communities.

Crime, for one, is the result of politicians using underrepresented communities as their scapegoats. These communities don't need political gibberish and useless rhetoric. They need more police, and more resources to maintain order and regain a foothold of socio-economic stability. Watch the evening news, members of the underrepresented communities, especially in D.C., New York, and most recently Colorado, begging for police presence. Politics has nothing to do with protecting the public. It should be a team effort, but it's always political. Every stakeholder has a contributory mission. But the burden really falls on elected officials and public administrators. Their sole mission… set the stage and create policy that will be in the best interests of the people and ensure the fidelity of government.

But the community also has a vested interest in protecting their own. Where does the community assume the responsibility for controlling crime? Where does the community encourage their children to be law abiding citizens? Where are the role models? Where is the community pride and personal responsibility? The reality has remained consistent across decades. Violent crime remains situated in underserved communities. Self-imploding in a failed socio-economic bubble. How and can that be resolved? Yes, by rolling up their sleeves and getting to work rebuilding the socio-economic foundation of the underrepresented communities.

SQF hit the tipping point in 2011, exceeding six hundred, fifty thousand SQF engagements. With only three percent of guns removed from the street. That should have triggered the community of stakeholders to do a deep dive, a one hundred percent program assessment. Was there an imbalance in enforcement? Unknown. What was known was that crime was down. And to the layperson the conclusion that it was a success. But the stakeholders failed. There was no conclusive analysis… program review… to determine levels of success or areas requiring improvement. By 2011 the unity of stakeholders was dissolved. There were two camps. Those who wanted to continue aggressive policing, and those who believed SQF was used to profile minorities. Failing to come together. Failing to achieve "Community Policing."

No one was willing to come to the table. The city unwilling to budge, happy to remain complacent, enjoying their mandated quotas. Expanding the wedge of community mistrust and adversarial relationships with the police. While criminals continued to exploit the underrepresented. Now politicians attempting to introduce ideological laws and policies to combat crime. Created in a liberal vacuum. Where racial equity and prosecution will drive the criminal justice system. Criminal justice driven by ideology. Good intentions or pandering political elites?

However, these "soft on crime" policies have not led to curtailment of violent crime. Regardless of the smoke and mirrors portrayed in crime statistics. There are extenuating circumstances that create those magical figures. Talk to the people in Harlem, Bedford Stuyvesant, Southeast D.C., Baltimore, St. Louis and Chicago. Political skewed statistics are doing nothing to stop the violence. Reports of daily shootings, normally the top story. Oblivious to parents begging for police protection and action to reduce violent crime.

Less aggressive policing equals less arrests and less incarcerations of minorities. Policing by racial equity. Yes, there is a huge disparity in the numbers of blacks incarcerated in the United States. Once an individual crosses over to the dark side and commits a homicide, assault, carjacking, robbery, there is no crossing back. An individual choice. And that's a personal decision, not one that has anything to do with race. And that's reality.

What's also reality is that the responsibility to provide the discipline, responsibility and accountability goes right back to parents, family, teachers, clergy and positive mentors. And the glaring failure of politicians. Not the police. One current policy in Chicago is engaging in less foot chases.[35] Less foot chases equals less apprehensions equals more perps on the streets committing crimes. The NYC council, in 2023 directed what is no more than a DEI playbook for police reform. A resolution directing specific special interest groups that have been unfairly treated by the police be given a golden ticket, free from prosecution. That enforcing the law on these groups is a discriminatory police practice. Reflected in a City Council Resolution.

"The Resolution" the product of a months-long engagement process through the NYC Police Reform and Reinvention Collaborative. Spanning nearly one hundred meetings and town halls, including nine public listening sessions. The Collaborative sought testimony and feedback from a broad range of New Yorkers, including; CBOs, advocacy groups, members of clergy, racial justice advocates, cure violence providers, youth groups and youth voices, ethnic and religious organizations, BIDs and small business owners, non-profits, LGBTQIA+ community leaders, the deaf and hard-of-hearing community, people with disabilities, tenants' associations, shelter-based and affordable housing communities and providers, people involved in the justice system, crime victims, policy experts, prosecutors and oversight bodies.

The one segment of the NYC population not represented to receive any special exemption… the working-class taxpaying citizens. Mayor Bill de Blasio affirming police attacks on underrepresented communities. Openly stating the reason for these reforms… cops are racists. "These reforms will confront centuries of over policing in communities of color and strengthen the bonds between police and community." Negating the unbiased facts reported in CompStat. And how has that worked out? Political ideology overriding the safety and quality of life of citizens.

Alvin Bragg has been accused of being "soft on crime." Bragg's position has been to reduce the number of prosecutions, and he has issued a memo saying that he would not prosecute multiple violent crimes and eliminate quality of life crimes, including prostitution, trespassing, resisting arrest, and most misdemeanors. Bragg has pushed back on those calling him soft on

---

[35] Opinion | The Chicago Model for Democrats (msn.com)

crime, telling CBS New York such accusations are "not accurate."[36] Intentionally failing to prosecute violations of the New York State penal law. Similarly in other urban cities across the country similar legal reforms have been implemented.

The stage was set. The new norm of daily shootings, violence, open air drug markets, street prostitution, the pungent smell of weed, and feces everywhere you turn. From Grand Central Station to the Theater District. With the influx of close to one hundred thousand illegals, city shelters overrun, trash, assaults, drugs, property destruction ignored. Another day in the city and happening across the country. This author believes that the downward spiral has gone too far and needs to be reversed. The nation's cities are engaged in urban warfare. Police reforms useless in the street. Politicians openly demonstrate their contempt for public safety. Rather than living in "Mayor or Governors Mansions", every politician should be required to live in the communities they represent. No security details, no special privilege. Live among your constituents, live their lives, experience their challenges, fears, and frustration. And you can't leave until problems are fixed or you're voted out of office.

What is reality for working class, taxpaying citizens… gangs still rule the streets. Drive by shootings will continue to take the lives of innocent men, women, and children every day. Arrested and released under *no cash bail*. Violent offenders back on the street. Will police reforms change the socio-economic conditions of underrepresented communities? Underrepresented communities have been ridden with poverty, poor education, and poor housing for decades. The cities forgotten. Caught in the eternal revolving door. Scapegoats of failed political administrations for perpetuity.

The cities governed by Mayors Bowser, Johnson, and Adams are no more than failed non-governmental organizations (NGOs). A picture of socialism. Resources controlled and directed by the government, sanctuary cities overrun by crime and illegals. The will of the party not of the people. And in 2024 a new criminal element… fascist agitators spewing religious hatred. Unchecked, they roam freely, supported by once revered centers of education, now ideological havens of socialism. These agitators, many who are clueless, destroying property, spewing threats and antisemite hate. Mob mentality. Just like the Nazi rise to power in the 1930s. The police unable to quell these mobs, hindered by politicians, who exacerbate political rhetoric. While sanctuary cities boast of their DEI leadership. Mayor Adams proudly boasting of his NYC "Chocolate" city council.[37] And in December of 2024 his Chocolate city council, and police department dropping like flies. His inner circle and the mayor indicted on charges of bribery and other yet to be released crimes.

Race politics at the expense of New York's citizens. The city returning to the Crime and Welfare state of the 1970s. Dismantling a once safe city. Violence begets violence. Illegals committing brazen crimes against citizens… and against the police. Citizens living in fear. And New York and all sanctuary cities are spending billions on free rides for illegals. Who wouldn't want to come into these cities, contribute absolutely nothing and be on permanent city welfare.

---

[36] Who is Alvin Bragg? What to know about the Manhattan D.A. weighing charges against Trump - CBS News
[37] https://www.msn.com/en-us/news/opinion/mayor-adams-plays-the-race-card-again-letters-to-the-editor-feb-9-2024/ar-BB1hZXZf?ocid=social share

45

Fentanyl flooding cities from the southern border, killing thousands. Blue sanctuary cities declared "an open city" by politicians.[38] (a town that has been abandoned, that the government will not defend, i.e., Crown Heights, East Harlem, Bedford Stuyvesant, the South Bronx.). National open cities, Chicago, D.C., Minneapolis, St. Louis, New Orleans, Aurora, Memphis, and Louisville. How's that going?

---

[38] http://www.dictionary.com/

Chapter 10 – Community Policing

The goal of community policing was to create partnerships between the police and the community. An innovative approach to unifying the community and the police. Co-producers   working in concert to introduce innovative change for safer and secure communities. Both groups working to capitalize on forming a relationship that emphasizes the skills of both groups to improve the living conditions of the neighborhood. Collaborations that not only work to reduce crime but instill confidence in the joint effort to reduce the fear of being a victim of crime. Is this strategy relevant in 2024? Will it be in 2025 and beyond?

It is called "deliberative democratic theory."[39] It stresses interaction between the community and police to affect public safety. Providing the framework that supports the belief that police should be more responsive and accountable to the citizenry and, more importantly, that the police should work to secure greater input and participation from community residents.

New York City's goal was always unity with the community. In a bold move to close the gap of mistrust between the community and police, the NYPD reintroduced the community police officer program. Commonly referred to as the Community Patrol Officer Program (CPOP). CPOP in the early 80s was innovative, designed as a problem-solving cooperative. Changing what is now "mobile response to calls for service." Bringing back the neighborhood patrol officer… the "beat cop." These officers take special interest in their neighborhoods as they identify and blend with the community. Armed with an understanding of police intelligence from the local precinct and community order-maintenance problems. Fully assimilated. Many officers from these communities. Well versed in the issues the communities face.

Over a four-year period, the program expanded to all of NYC's seventy five precincts. What became a cornerstone program. The program focused on the officers' effectiveness in the implementation of their new roles, the obstacles encountered, and the communities' response. The evaluation consisted of interviews with "beat officers", their supervisors, commanding officers, and community residents. CPOP unfortunately was short lived. Lack of community involvement, limited resources, and command support and the introduction of mobile policing led to its slow curtailment.

Changing procedures for calls for service… the nail in the coffin. Changing a "street presence" to a mobile response where officers were pinpointed to a crime scene. They investigated, interviewed witnesses, compiled a police report, and returned to the precinct. Extremely limiting police community interaction (buy-in). The relationship between the community and police strained.

The next cornerstone of today's NYPD is Neighborhood Policing, introduced in 2015. A comprehensive crime-fighting strategy built on improved communication and collaboration between local police officers and community residents (sound familiar). The goal… to strengthen bonds between officers and the neighborhoods they serve while enhancing crime-fighting capabilities. Neighborhood Policing greatly increases connectivity and engagement

---

[39] DELIBERATIVE DEMOCRATIC THEORY | Annual Reviews

with the community without diminishing, and, in fact, improving the NYPD's crime-fighting capabilities.

The NYPD has long encouraged officers to strengthen bonds with the communities they patrol, but past practice in precincts left little time or opportunity for true community engagement. By 2018 the program was active in every residential precinct. Yet resources like CPOP were slowly re-tasked to other priorities (counterterrorism).

The current initiative in NYC, Project Reset is a diversion program that reassesses response to first-time, low-level criminal offenses. Originally launched in select precincts in Manhattan and Brooklyn in February 2015, Project Reset sought to reintegrate minors (ages sixteen and seventeen) into society by enabling them to undergo community-based, rehabilitative intervention in lieu of criminal prosecution. With support from the Center for Court innovation and the Osborne Association, the program was developed to hold young people accountable for their actions, while simultaneously identifying social deficiencies, addressing them, and avoiding incarceration and the societal implications that often follow a criminal record.

At the point of arrest, a police officer would inform the young person when he or she is eligible to take part in Project Reset. Participation in the program is voluntary, and the rehabilitative intervention is provided through group workshops, community service, and individual and group counseling sessions. Participants must have been sixteen or seventeen years of age, must have been a first-time offender, arrested for a nonviolent misdemeanor, and have no outstanding cases against them. Within the first six months of operation, ninety-eight percent of participants successfully completed their restorative intervention and avoided formal case processing. The question needs to be asked… is the program still viable? Or have resources and the juveniles this program was meant to help, now the juveniles who are committing most of the violent crime? What's the answer Mr. Mayor?

In 2024 the challenges the NYPD faces remain as diverse as the city. The influx of illegal migrants, explosion of violent crime, legalization of marijuana, criminals facing little, or no consequence have brought a cloud over the city. And cities across the nation. Police departments are suffering from staffing gaps. Departments are in constant flux. Can community policing be accomplished in this era of *defund the police*? And how effective can community policing be, now and in the future, if the culture in the community remains police mistrust? Therein lies the real measurement of success or failure of community policing.

RAND Report

Police Commissioner Dermet Shea in late 2018, requested the RAND corporation perform an independent evaluation to measure the public's trust in police. One part of this evaluation involved two surveys that the RAND Corporation administered in November 2020 and May 2021. The surveys asked people in diverse communities to respond to more than eighty questions measuring three essential elements of police-community relations: engagement, trustworthiness, and guardianship. This research is part of an ongoing evaluation of the NYPD's Neighborhood Policing philosophy.

The overall goal of the study was to better understand perspectives on the police in NYC's neighborhoods, and to help guide their efforts to strengthen relationships with the communities they serve. Key findings included:

- About two-thirds of respondents report positive attitudes toward police in their neighborhoods.
- In general respondents who live in areas with lower violent crime agreed more often with positive statements about police than those who live in areas with higher violent crime.

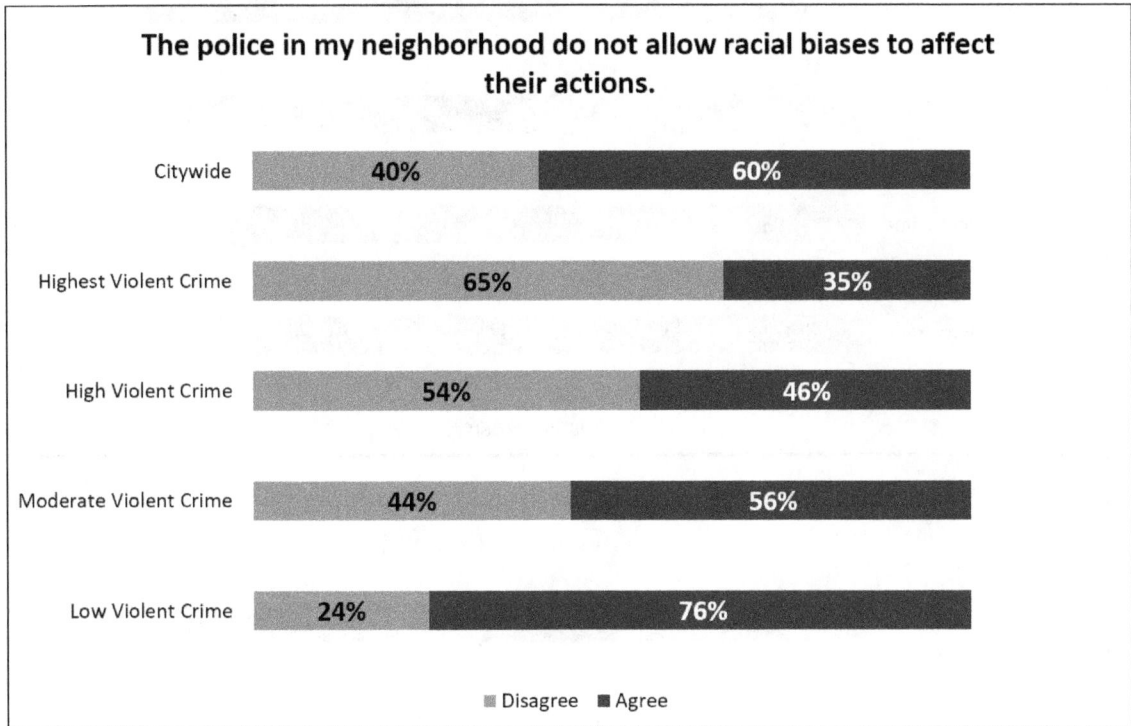

The police in my neighborhood do not allow racial biases to affect their actions.

Category	Disagree	Agree
Citywide	40%	60%
Highest Violent Crime	65%	35%
High Violent Crime	54%	46%
Moderate Violent Crime	44%	56%
Low Violent Crime	24%	76%

■ Disagree ■ Agree

-

The police in my neighborhood make decisions based on facts and the law and not on their own personal opinions.

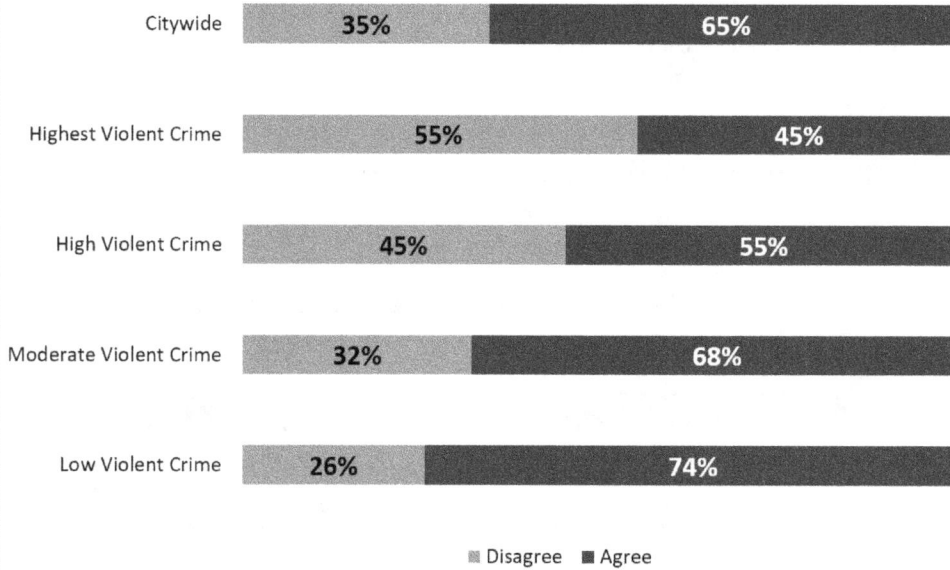

	Disagree	Agree
Citywide	35%	65%
Highest Violent Crime	55%	45%
High Violent Crime	45%	55%
Moderate Violent Crime	32%	68%
Low Violent Crime	26%	74%

■ Disagree ■ Agree

The police in my neighborhood treat people fairly.

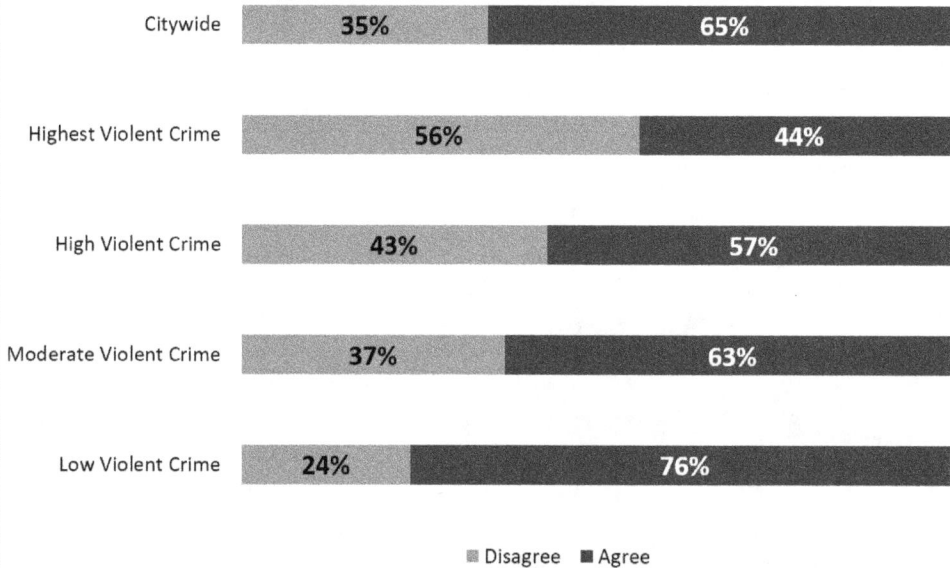

	Disagree	Agree
Citywide	35%	65%
Highest Violent Crime	56%	44%
High Violent Crime	43%	57%
Moderate Violent Crime	37%	63%
Low Violent Crime	24%	76%

■ Disagree ■ Agree

Table 4 - RAND Report Findings

The RAND Survey results were not surprising. High crime areas report less favorable interactions. While low crime areas report favorable interactions. From the community policing standpoint that statistically reflects a possible correlation to community police effectiveness. With limited resources, precinct commanders utilize every officer to mitigate criminal activity. High crime areas place a burden on depleted resources, with community officers being re-missioned to patrol. Taking a toll on the continuity of officers to affect the community/police bond. And in 2024 being mobilized to deal with the influx of illegal migrants, and college protesters wreaking havoc across the city.

The RAND survey was a non-biased evaluation, one that provided an excellent "Report Card" for the city. But that was in 2018. The impact… a solid tool for the Police and City Administration to reflect and assess community policing efforts. Fast forward to 2024 and beyond. In an era where modifications of laws have encouraged violent crime without accountability (enforcement and prosecution) what will be the effect on community policing? What would the findings of a RAND survey be today, as the city crumbles under the weight of failed law enforcement policies and uncontrolled violence?

Two ad hoc reports were also commissioned by the city to assess the opinion of SQF in the communities most affected. An ad hoc public opinion study of SQF strategy was conducted by surveying the perceptions of pedestrians in NYC during the summer of 2014 and then again in 2023. The original 2014 survey and the one conducted almost nine years later in 2023 were almost identical. As expected, Black, Hispanic youth and older minorities were more negative about SQF and law enforcement than Caucasians. Although positive opinions were reported in other groups. Also, specific characteristics had a dramatic effect on SQF opinions. Positive comments from individuals with higher levels of education, full time employment, higher income, married, and having children. Never having experienced an SQF event and personal acquaintance with a police officer. Negative opinions from those individuals from single parent households, minimal education, unemployed, and receiving public assistance. The trend has not changed for decades.

Both the RAND and Ad Hoc reports are almost identical in their conclusions. What has been the impact of these results? These reports, while providing substantial evidence from both ends of the socio-economic spectrum… failed to include input from patrol officers. The below statement is from one minority officer and his interaction with the community. Not the apples and oranges conclusions provided in the RAND report. Most officers I interviewed held the same opinion.

"Some of these communities, the community culture is messed up. Selling drugs, violence, living on welfare, having kids and the crap with no fathers keeps going. The other crap, drugs, poverty, and the other social problems I can't fix, that's politicians' fault and the people who live in the community."

A perspective from where the rubber meets the road. This statement was based on the officer's interaction during the SQF Era. Fast forwarded to today and nothing has changed. With politicians banging the drum of *defund the police*, and the police remaining in a respond and report mode… the perfect storm. A stage for continued anarchy, chaos, and zero consequences for violent criminals. With the police in a reactive, not pro-active culture.

Procedural Justice

The NYPD also sought the aid of the RAND Corporation to gain clarity in understanding the validity, or lack of public claims of police discrimination. At first glance, the raw data showed large racial disparities; eighty-nine percent of stops involved minorities, noting that fifty-three percent of stops involved African Americans, twenty-nine percent Hispanic, eleven percent White, and three percent Asians. Furthermore, forty-five percent of African Americans and Hispanics were frisked compared to twenty-nine percent of Whites. Yet, White suspects were seventy percent more likely to have a weapon. The RAND Corporation evaluated all street encounters that occurred during 2006 and approached the data from three perspectives.

1. Analysis of external benchmarks
2. Analysis of internal benchmarks
3. Outcomes of the SQF incidents reviewed.

The RAND Corporation's analysis described the difficulty in developing valid external benchmarks under SQF circumstances. Rand used two external methods that included the racial distribution of arrestees and persons identified as crime suspects. With the last considered the most credible measure. Verifying that black pedestrians were stopped at a rate twenty to thirty percent less often than expected. Based on their racial representation in this category, Hispanics were stopped five to ten percent more often than expected.

The arrest benchmarking method found that blacks were stopped at the expected rate with Hispanics slightly above. The third and least dependable model based on residential census showed blacks were stopped at a rate fifty percent higher than expected. Surprisingly, internal staff and procedures analysis resulted in an overall finding that flagged only one-half percent of the total <u>NYPD workforce as potentially acting in a racist manner</u>.

The result found that whites were frisked slightly less often than blacks at twenty-nine and thirty-three percent respectively, in similar circumstances. Blacks were frisked slightly more often than whites at rates of forty-six and forty-two percent, respectively. White suspects were slightly more likely to receive a summons, Black suspects were slightly more likely to be arrested, and force was less likely to be used on whites, as compared to blacks, at fifteen and sixteen percent, respectively. The results of the analysis are highly credible. This analysis equivocally dispelled the claims of discrimination and racial police behaviors. And to provide reinforcement… RAND's study was totally "unbiased."

Where are we today? Now, during the era of *Defund the Police*, there has not been "One" external or internal study on Stop Question and Frisk and broken windows. Just political rhetoric, while crime spirals out of control, at the public's expense. All generated by political and media sensationalism. Not the facts. When will municipalities consider the facts? Is that even possible?

The country remains divided by race. And the stark reality is communities of color remain underrepresented. As they unfortunately have for decades, with one very visible fact. Those communities who are historically victims of violent crime, and on the opposite end of the socio-economic scale, remain under siege not by white conservatives, but by minority politicians who promise and pander to their minority constituents for the almighty vote. Then when elected, do absolutely nothing to change their socio-economic condition. Cases in point: Bowser of D.C., Lightfoot and Johnson of Chicago, Cantrell of New Orleans, Adams of NYC, Dickens of Atlanta, Breed of San Francisco and Thoa of Oakland. Great at lies, inuendo and no action. Their communities ravaged, cesspools of crime. Their response… the political two step. Crime decimating their communities. And in some cases, using statistics that are skewed for their advantage to demonstrate drops in crime.

The RAND report also projected a disturbing conclusion. Their report concluded that in their analysis of two hundred, ninety-seven geographically diverse neighborhoods, data indicated Blacks and Hispanics were statistically more likely to commit crimes. The data was consistent with assertions made by the NYC Police Commissioner at the time; Howard Safir (1996 – 2000). As he responded to claims of criminal racial disparity. Mayor Bloomberg stated that the known racial makeup of criminal offenders provided the basis of police procedures, not racial bias. This statement was also consistent with the testimony of NYPD officials during the trial of *Floyd v. The City of New York*. And the data identified in CompStat (1992-2013).

The population and racial census of the Rikers Island Prison in NYC were used as an index to compare SQF police activity regarding the claims of racial disparity. The incarcerated population during this time was ninety-one percent minority: fifty-six percent Black and thirty-five percent Hispanic. Comparatively, the stops recorded by the NYPD were fifty-three percent Black and thirty-one percent Hispanic. The findings provided statistically significant evidence consistent with the RAND Corporation's analysis, public statements and court testimony indicating the SQF procedure was not racially biased. Data solely based on arrests of individuals committing crimes in racial populations of geographically clustered neighborhoods (Brownsville, Bedford Stuyvesant, Crown Heights, Jamaica, and the Bronx). And in 2025 the trend has not deviated. Not subject to New York, but across the nation.

Procedural Justice or Procedural Injustice

During the 2013 trial of *Floyd v. New York City*, Michael Bloomberg, the Mayor of NYC, expressed the opinion that the policing procedures of the NYPD, including the SQF strategy, had saved thousands of citizens' lives and promoted safer communities. During the same trial, the U.S. Justice Department filed a statement with the court with an opposing position. Indicating that unlawful and aggressive police strategies were not only inappropriate and unnecessary but detrimental to the overall goals of crime reduction.

Both arguments pursuing to identify the best procedures to build trust with the community and develop police legitimacy. The ruling was in favor of the NYPD. What is the state of Police legitimacy in the *defund the police* era? Is there police legitimacy? A difficult answer. You decide… with policies of *no cash bail*, minimal prosecutions, the police scapegoats for political agendas. How does this demonstrate police legitimacy and build community trust?

Procedural justice or injustice revisits the application of the broken windows theory. Reiterating the purpose and subsequent value of maintaining order in public areas to improve the quality of life of citizens and reduce opportunities for crime. Emphasizing that the broken windows "theory" is entirely separate from SQF policing. The broken windows theory is an approach to reduce physical and social disorder including disorderly and illegal behaviors. It is not an enforcement tool.

Order maintenance policing,[40] including SQF are the enforcement tactics. Often equated with rigid tactics evolving from the broken windows theory. Yes, building community relations and developing trust is a priority mission of the police department, but not the number one priority. The number one priority of the police is to enforce the law and protect citizens.

What do politicians use as their theoretical foundations to improve the socio-economic dilemma of their respective communities? Unfounded promises and lies... politics 101. Unfortunately, since the police are on the front lines, interacting with the community, they bear the brunt of community frustration. They are the whipping posts. On the blame line for the faults of political indecision and poor socio-economic conditions. Politicians far removed from their districts, their constituents, and the problems they created. One of the biggest examples in New York is Alexandria Ocasio-Cortez, AKA AOC. No congressional office in her district, circling the wagons with the elites in D.C. her constituents forgotten... until election time. The same dysfunction that existed in the 1970s. On steroids in 2024. Political solutions... divide and conquer through race politics, lies and mistrust.

During the SQF era the NAACP, the Vera Institute, and Dr. Jones-Brown, a staunch civil rights activist from John Jay University argued that many black youths, mainly males, complained of being stopped multiple times. Creating emotional damage to these young men, their families, and their communities. Repeated procedural episodes of unfairness further contributed to the long-term result of instilling an unwillingness in citizens to contribute to and cooperate with law enforcement officers.

Personal health was also correlated with the use of SQF in NYC The likelihood of young males developing symptoms consistent with trauma and anxiety have been directly tied to intrusive or perceived unfair SQF encounters. Diabetes, blood pressure, asthma and obesity, related diseases attributed to SQF. While there may be validity to the presentation of direct correlation to SQF, the reality is well documented, that these same health concerns are hereditary and causes of the lack of basic health care. And have been inherent to the black community for generations. The question is who is responsible for individual health...?

Where are we in 2025? Police presence and staffing is at a minimum. Political underdogs. Recruiting in some departments still scrutinized to meet DEI quotas. The steady, relentless revolving door of young black males in and out of court back on the streets under no cash bail. Free to resume acts of violence. Soft on Crime policies pandering to minorities... a miserable failure. Gun violence out of control. Urban cities returning to the days of the Wild West. Shootouts... the accepted way to settle disputes. The scales of justice tarnished.

Families absorbed by fear. Scared to go outside, their children open targets of drive-by shootings. Schools and playgrounds, once safe havens, now battlefields. Daily shootings and carnage a common occurrence. Fear and unwillingness to cooperate with law enforcement a pendulum. Communities demanding law enforcement take criminals off the street. And in

---

[40] Order Maintenance Policing | SpringerLink

underrepresented communities no one is screaming racism, they are screaming for police protection. Politicians who are using racism to bolster and cover up their ineptness.

And there is a cultural issue that remains pushed to the curb. It's a huge issue and mainly occurring in underrepresented communities. This is insanity. The dysfunctional family. Unfortunately, the word dysfunctional is the correct definition of the problem. "A dysfunctional family is a family in which conflict, misbehavior, and often child neglect or abuse on the part of individual parents occurs continuously and regularly. Children that grow up in such families may think such a situation is normal."

A continued cultural problem precipitated in black households… the lack of fathers. Sociologists have identified the outcomes of fatherless black homes. They have long advocated the importance of a "traditional family." Fathers are a huge influence in setting the life path of their children. They are the rock… providing guidance, discipline, and mentorship for their children. They set the stage to teach their children individual and social responsibility, a work ethic and respect for others. Black fathers over the course of decades continue to be unable to perform their "core" mission. Yet while this remains a significant cultural issue, the traditional Black family continues to be attacked by DEI and woke pundits. Ideological garbage that fathers are no longer an integral part of moral and social development. But where are the fathers? The result is not encouraging and what is the path for many of the children from fatherless homes… incarceration, unemployment, alcoholism, drawn to crime. Adult black males removed from their children's lives. Their children and children's children caught in a never-ending roller coaster of despair and hopelessness.

Strong Black women assuming the role of father and mother. Black youths swept up by the streets… gangs replacing their fathers. The U.S. Census bureau reported that seventy-four percent of all white children below the age of eighteen live with both parents. Only thirty-eight percent of black children reside in a two-parent home. Single family homes in underrepresented communities remain at a disadvantage economically, educationally, suffering from poor health. All contributing to undesirable impacts on quality of life. Another distractor… potential mates for minority women dwindled due to incarceration. Resulting in further economic and housing struggles. A revolving door of dysfunction. Generations lost.[41]

A 2017 study[42] captured the opinions of one hundred ten African American and Hispanic male and female adults living in high crime areas of NYC to measure the levels of trust in police and their willingness to cooperate. The survey's results indicated that many participants displayed an unwillingness to cooperate with police. The current situation in 2025… nothing has changed. Consistent over decades, and generations. The criminal justice system from the street to the courtroom remains adversarial. And that trust will not be changed with racial equity or political rhetoric. It will be achieved by sincerity and a return to "beat cop" policing. Community involvement, establishing safe public spaces for everyone. Most importantly, getting all stakeholders on board. Unify public safety as NYC did during the 90s. Working together acting fairly and respectfully. The solution… return to broken windows policing.

---

[41] Census Bureau: Higher Percentage of Black Children Live with Single Mothers | AFRO American Newspapers
[42] Legitimacy Policing In Depth | RAND

When that occurs, there may be a chance, and only a chance to return to the expectation of law enforcement and the community working together as a team. Purging the barriers of mistrust. The police perform their duties with fairness, and effectiveness. Preventing and reducing crime, preserving the safety of all citizens, while maintaining legitimacy and the trust of those they serve. That's the ideological platform. Reality however demonstrates that in this current state of war, this is a bridge too far. And it will never be one hundred percent harmonious. Political barriers with the continued pursuit of *defund the police* and sanctuary cities. The media skewed in their negative optics of the police, operating on a basis of misinformation, attempting to influence public opinion. Propaganda. Creating a police reluctance to actively enforce the law. Proliferating community mistrust. Inherently in this balancing act, what input does the community have in contributing to law enforcement policy? From a limited review of the top five cities with the highest statistics of violent crime… the answer is none. How can any police policy ignore input from the community? This same trend is not only an abomination in the United States but across the globe. The balancing act takes place daily. The communities ignored in acts of intentional political segregation. In NYC, Chicago, St. Louis, what should be an interwoven blanket of unity between the community of stakeholders; community/politicians/police have dwindled. Eroding police legitimacy.

Procedural justice or injustice? It's a dangerous political pendulum with the safety and security of our nation hanging in the balance.

Chapter 11 – Political Influence

Community Policing was a fantastic initiative, but like SQF it was impacted by politicians that opened the door for illegals, eliminated zero tolerance infractions, introduced *no cash bail*, and catch and release. With SQF the tipping point was the introduction of *quota* mandated UF 250 stops[43]. For each SQF encounter a UF 250 had to be prepared. Turned into the precinct. Rolled up and provided as part of the weekly CompStat statistics. This placed officers between a rock and hard place. As they were directed to provide designated numbers of UF 250s. The quota.

In 2024 the City Council is proposing in their twisted political perspective *encounter reports*. A form to record police encounters that captures ethnicity, race and sexual affirmation. The underlying intent… to demonstrate that the NYPD are systemically racist. Supporting the council's progressive agenda, not targeting criminals, but the NYPD. Attempting to provide conclusions that the NYPD targets minority and diverse groups (Black, Hispanic, LGBTQ). The underlying political platform of race politics. All in line with the police reforms introduced in 2021[44]. A plan to confront racialized policing in the NYPD. In essence holding the police accountable for every failed socio-economic policy in NYC. New Yorks City politicians openly declaring war on the police.

A far cry from the original intent of SQF… allowing officer discretion through the lens of *probable* suspicion. Regardless, fifty-three percent of NYPD officers constitute a multitude of minority and diverse groups. The end state is already reality… the encounter reports will be manipulated to prove that the NYPD is systemically racist. The result… officers will limit encounters. The fear of baseless accusations, media sensationalism. All filling a political agenda. Ferguson effect on steroids. Citizens are vulnerable to index and property crimes. The effect on the city… limited interaction and delays in response to calls for service. Widening the gap of community trust Officers with targets on their back, political puppets. Until a young child is murdered or a heinous murder committed. Then there will be a time out, while the call for police services rings from the hypocrites in the city council.

During the SQF era, politicians achieved crime reduction through what became no more than a quota system. The more stops performed, the better the political panorama. But how would officers select individuals to be stopped? And how would officers execute what became no more than quota harvesting? From officer discretion… to a fishing exhibition. The fishing pond… minority communities. The UF 250s… the bait. Officers "fishing" to meet quotas. And UF 250 stops had nothing to do with removing guns from the street… it was an abomination of SQF. It was a mayoral decision to keep up political appearances.

Examining "License to Fish"

Officers were unanimous that once politicians mandated *policing by the numbers* the program veered off track. The UF 250 (record of Stop) removed officer discretion. Officers had to go out

---

[43] http://blog.danwin.com/files/images/uf250-2011-excerpt.png
[44] City Council Passes Comprehensive Police Reform Resolution | City of New York (nyc.gov)

on patrol and *fish* for individuals to search. No longer employing probable suspicion and officer discretion, based on experience and judgement. Driven by the City Administration. What is provided below is officers' perceptions of their experiences.

> *"OK, crime is high; we need more stops to bring crime down. Now crime is down and we're increasing the stops? Or like I said before, let's say when it started, and this is just hypothetical, when it started, one out of every three people you stopped had a weapon or was wanted for something, one out of three. OK, now, when it's one out of nine, you must sit up there and go, we must stop doing this because now were stopping eight people for no reason."*

> *"When you're stopping seven or eight people, and you're letting them all go, at what point do you go, 'If I did something five times and it yielded nothing, I'm going to start reevaluating how I'm using that.' It's going to stop being, well, we know we can stop them, and we have a stop, question, and frisk, let's keep stopping. No, it's gonna be, 'I just stopped five people for nothing, or for whatever reason.' But it turned out to be nothing. I need to scale back so that I'm not stopping so many people for no reason."*

All the participants noted that regardless of the reduction in crime… to what the city determined were "acceptable numbers" by 2011 forced activity (UF 250s) to substantiate statistical enforcement was the standard police practice. And race was always the number one issue. Fact – the police did not create the racial problem… it was created by politicians. By mandating quotas, the police packed their fishing poles and went on patrol. Fishing excursions to harvest their catch. Unfortunately, where was the best place to go fishing (demographic), underrepresented communities, and young black men.

> *"If we saw black kids standing on the corner with their pants off their ass, were they criminals? No, they have a bad fashion sense. What is my reason for going in and stopping them? They're not doing anything wrong. It's not a crime to stand on the corner."*

> *"So, with stop, question, and frisk, at the onset, being a useful, good policing tool for what the intent was through broken windows. But it grew too big and got out of control with quotas. It just kept on going. It never got reassessed, nobody looked at the after and the impact of the program success."*

Was the decision to pursue forced quota harvesting effective? Did it have a negative impact, furthering a rift and loss of police legitimacy in the underrepresented communities? Political quota harvesting an attempt to maintain party agenda. In 2014, Mayor Bill de Blasio eliminated SQF. But license to fish was not curtailed. The new targeted catch… the police. Blue fishing exploded in 2020. The bait overzealous policing and systemic racism. To pay for their sins, politicians created criminal friendly policies. *No Cash Bail* – releasing criminals, for anything less than murder, manslaughter, rape, assault (only if the victim received major injuries). And other crime identified in Alvin Braggs first day in office memorandum to his staff.

Reducing prosecution of violent felonies, reducing charges to misdemeanors. Eliminating prosecution for low level crimes (zero tolerance – fare beating, public urination, street prostitution). With one single goal… reduce the disparate prosecution of persons of color and reduce the disproportionate incarceration rates. Appeasement. With these new zero prosecution policies, what has changed? Violent crime has risen in underrepresented communities. On TV, in the media and on the street, criminal statistics continue to point to one demographic committing most violent crimes… young black males. No conjecture, no racial bias… fact.

Politicians, especially black politicians, refusing to accept these facts. It would tarnish their stellar, honest, selfless service to the people's image. Under current blue city policies criminals are processed through the revolving criminal justice door, returned to the streets emboldened to continue their rein of crime. Zero tolerance in reverse.

Officers provided parallel responses to the reasons why they believed SQF changed. The preponderance of officer responses was almost identical… that SQF became a management tool directed by the police brass and politicians. Removing the ability of officers to effectively use their police skills and judgement to enforce the law.

"Initially, it (SQF) was a success; it became a failure because they put numbers on it. If they would've let cops go with their instincts, and most cops have good instincts. If it would've been done right, there would've been no lawsuits. But when you put pressure on somebody to do something, they tend to overstep their boundaries just to satisfy somebody else, so they don't get into trouble. I think it just became a numbers thing and just got out of control. Did we cross the line that in terms of people's liberties and civil liberties and stuff? Yes, I guess. But you know what, I just got a gun off the streets that was going to kill my cousin or my nephew, right?"

Officers caught in the political cross hairs. CompStat the golden calf. But once fishing quotas were mandated… community activists started pushing back. Officers being accused of over zealously targeting minority communities. It angered and pissed off the community. Especially when there was no legal foundation for a stop. No more than nuisance stops. But mandatory fishing quotas had not been curtailed, regardless that the pond dried up. Minority communities were justified in their anger and frustration.

Officers indicated a lack of faith and trust in information complied and released by CompStat. Officers indicated that they observed a difference in what they viewed as crime levels while they were working, and what was reflected in CompStat. Based on officer's perceptions they believed CompStat metrics were being modified.

"CompStat's always watered down."

"Crime is down that percent. Is it? Maybe? Who knows? Is it creative numbering? Is it that people are not calling the police, or what? It could be a factor of things.".

"It's added pressure, because when the mayor or other people get up at a press conference, what's the first thing they say? Crime is down this percent.".

One black officer noted that he perceived that even though CompStat figures indicated that crime was down:

"Crime has increased since 9/11. While we focus on 9/11, terrorism, what's going up? Local crimes. Gang violence. Crime against women and children, they've increased."

Aggressive policing unchanged. And community policing is moving in the wrong direction. Removing the beat cops and going to mobile policing. Responding to multiple calls, bouncing from one crime scene to another. The connection between the police and community eroded. Trying to maintain legitimacy not only in New York, but most departments across the country. Political interference creates an almost insurmountable challenge. Politicians are shifting millions from the police to social programs and the influx of illegals. Cops operating on a shoestring budget. The intentional police hatred spewed by politicians having a terrible consequence in the ability to recruit quality officers. The result failed public policy. Politicians who should be dedicated to selfless service, and representatives of the people... being one with self... self-serving.

Public Administrative theory calls for public programs to be reviewed every three to five years to ensure effectiveness. NYC ignored the basics of public administration. They had their own agenda. Even more so... are patrol officers, the subject matter experts included in policy reviews? Evaluation of SQF had gone awry with "fishing and quotas." Because bureaucrats and politicians did an armchair assessment, never having done a ride along. The city administration is happy with the status quo. And absolutely nothing can go wrong when you use numbers as your strategy to assess the effectiveness of the human condition. And minority officers the real pawns... caught in a vice. Displaying empathy and allegiance with the minority community, yet their sworn duty to enforce the law..

The "new urban normal." These communities resembling war zones. Shootings, robberies, snatch, and grabs, carjackings, assaults, drive bye's... just another day in urban America. In 2024 the public has had enough. A new outcry for law and order. Getting police back on the streets. For a return of SQF and active policing. Scared for their lives and the lives of their families. Yet there is still a political push back.

What is evident, SQF, was an effective public policy. It achieved its original intent of using probable suspicion to get guns off the street. Fact... crime was controlled. Police technology and statistically generated data was used to track and deploy officers to hot spots. The benefactors, the people of the City of New York and urban communities across the nation..

As politicians played the race game, misinformation and political bravado and propaganda replaced facts and reality. Regardless of the Maron Institute and RAND studies, politicians ignored their credible and factual findings. Rather, in this debilitating era of DEI and woke insanity, opponents of public safety, in attempts to hold onto political power, used their administrations to play the game of ideology. Clogging up the public safety system, placing unqualified DEI appointees in senior leadership positions at the federal, state, and local levels. No more than figureheads. Spewing "word salads" and vying for photo ops.

And today, politicians continue to deflect from tackling life and death issues. Playing the same rhetorical, pass the buck games. With the same results... underrepresented minority communities bearing the effects of violent crime, poverty, and socio-economic decline. The fallout... not only out of control violence, but the influx of unvetted, undocumented illegals who have arrived in NYC and other urban cities in mass. Stripping urban "sanctuary" cities of their resources. Costing billions. Politicians stripping emergency services, police, social service budgets, to house, feed and provide free medical care for illegals. Illegals openly attacking the police. And who's footing the bill... American citizens.

In November 2019, prior to the start of his democratic presidential campaign, NYC's Mayor Bloomberg issued an apology for his policy of stop and frisk. Speaking at a predominantly Black church in Brooklyn, he stated:

"Today I want you to know that I realized back then I was wrong … [and] I didn't understand that back then, the full impact that stops were having on the black and Latino communities."

During a February 2020 campaign event, Bloomberg further apologized for the practice, stating:.

"I should have acted sooner and faster to stop it, I didn't, and for that I apologize.".

Prior to his presidential campaign, Bloomberg had defended stop and frisk with vigor during his tenure as Mayor of the City of New York and on numerous occasions. Political sham. Mayor Giuliani never changed his position that stop, question and frisk… saved lives. In October 2013 he restated his position allowing the NYPD to change course "into a proactive police force" implementing broken windows policing. Criticizing stop, question and frisk under Bloomberg, defending his own use of the strategy, claiming, *"We were following… not race, we were following complaints … [and] the African American community was selecting for us who to go look for."* How prophetic, the black community partnering with the NYPD. Commonly known as… Community Policing.

In September 2016, then-presidential candidate Donald Trump expressed support for stop and frisk and claimed it *"worked incredibly well"* in NYC. In October 2018, as President of the United States, Trump claimed he instructed the Attorney General's office *"to work with local authorities [in Chicago] … and to strongly consider stop-and-frisk."* He also praised stop, question and frisk under Giuliani and claimed NYC *"went from an unacceptably dangerous city to one of the safest cities in the country."* According to a recent analysis by WalletHub, NYC was ranked the 113th safest city in the U.S. This 2019 survey compared one hundred, eighty-two urban cities. Chicago, in the bottom sixteen percent of safe cities, with pro-active policing restricted by political stupidity. Like after birth. Chicago reported forty shootings on Memorial Day weekend 2024. Just another weekend in Windy City.

Catch and Release – *No Cash Bail*

Broken Windows has been studied, taken apart and placed under a microscope. The issues of disproportionate enforcement in minority communities, under the Obama Administration became the rallying cry to turn away from broken windows. Generating a national effort to eliminate the police practice of Stop Question and Frisk. The death of Michael Brown in Ferguson, Missouri in 2014 sparked the national fervor on the war on police. Eric Garner's death in NYC and the death of George Floyd opened the flood gates for liberals and progressives to lead a national movement to transform law enforcement and even eliminate the police. In Ferguson, the Department of Justice assuming oversight on the police department, immediately introducing the elimination of bail for minority offenders, unable to post bond. Instituting a revolving door of no consequences for criminals. Released on "desk appearance tickets" back into the community. The beginning of the national acceptance of no cash bail. Spreading across the nation like wildfire. Perpetrators, going through the revolving door, returned to the community. Still in place in many urban communities. Communities living in fear while animals roam the streets.

"Catch and Release," a phrase originated in recreational fishing over a century ago, refers to releasing fish after capture. Now applied to the practice of processing and releasing illegal immigrants detained at the border without proper vetting. Releasing illegals into the community with an order to appear at a future date for an immigration hearing, as an alternative to detention. Current figures speculate that close to eighty-five percent of those released have disappeared into the interior of the United States. Whereabouts unknown[45]. Americans denied our rights to Life, Liberty and the Pursuit of Happiness. The Declaration of Independence, the foundation of our nation, is non-applicable for illegals. DEI, radical left-wing policies circumventing and ignoring federal immigration law.

The crime rate in the past three years with the elimination of SQF and broken windows has skyrocketed. Smoke and mirrors, duck and cover political policies. Turnstile jumping (fare beating) is a common occurrence, not enforced in NYC and D.C. This victimless crime, not victimless… costing millions in lost revenue annually. And who bears the brunt of zero enforcement… the taxpayer. Homeless everywhere… roaming the streets. Harassing and assaulting innocent civilians, the smell of urine and feces, permeate the homeless encampments. A new dawn. The new daily course of life in these public health cesspools. The normal aroma of NYC, Washington, D.C., Baltimore, New Orleans, Chicago. Taking the cake… San Francisco… homeless encampments dot the parks and empty lots in residential neighborhoods. On City streets homeless openly urinating and defecating, the stench horrific. Needles adorn the street like shells on a beach. Not what the founding fathers intended. Politicians ignore the threats to public safety..

It's time to return to common sense policing. Replace catch and release and no cash bail with "Arrest and Prosecute." SQF was not discriminatory. It became politicized. A sound police tool that was mis- utilized and manipulated. Law enforcement took criminals off the street. They made arrests based on the validity of probable suspicion and probable cause. We are on the precipice; the pendulum can swing either way. We'll either sink or swim. Our national security depends on it. What will our future hold?

Since 2020 these no consequence policies have led to an open season on police officers. Two NYPD Officers were brutally attacked in broad daylight, on February 8th, 2024. Seven violent illegal thugs knocked officers to the ground, kicking and punching them. Alvin Bragg the Manhattan DA called these attacks "despicable" and "heinous." Yet six of the seven charged with assault in the second degree, were released without bail. Disappearing into the labyrinth of the sea of illegals. Criminals face reduced charges or zero prosecution. And in 2025, urban cities still have no cash bail laws on the books, with no intentions to correct this insanity. All while politicians praise each other for their criminal justice reforms. Politicians, especially in New York governor Hochul with their heads in the clouds. Like Ocasio, Leticia James, tripping over their tongues, unable to piece together a cognitive thought. Their ridiculous soft on crime policies, race baiting the direct cause of criminal chaos and anarchy. Politicians are guilty of not only collusion but as co-conspirators. They are the true perpetrators yet never held accountable for the death and pain they cause in urban communities.

---

[45] Breaking Down the Immigration Figures - FactCheck.org

Chapter 12 – Organizational Culture

The NYPD is the largest police department in the world with approximately 35,000 sworn officers. Like most police departments, the NYPD is a paramilitary organization that is complex and hierarchical. The chain-of-command structure provides policies, directives, and procedures that are imposed through the ranks of officers by the Police Commissioner. Policy approval and oversight is executed by a civilian Mayoral Administration. The police department setting the stage for officers to affect sound policing is dependent on an organization's culture. Positive or negative, culture is the invisible attitude of the organization.

Affected by external conditions, the organizational culture is people. Policing within the diverse communities in a city the size of NYC is challenging. Now the once proud culture and aura of being a NYPD officer has been shattered by leftist politicians using the police as their scapegoats for failed policies. But unlike politicians, cops just can't leave and go home. They are bound to police the streets and protect her citizens.

A public perception of the NYPD is that department organizational culture is racially biased. This has been investigated, and unfounded. Especially with the change in the department diverse make up of fifty-two percent. Each of us has moral and ethical values. But once we transition within the boundaries of the organization, we assume the organizational culture. Many community leaders and politicians believe in the stigma that there is abject racism in law enforcement. Are the police able to fairly enforce the law for all citizens? Is there bias in the organizational culture? Let's take a deep dive into this.

Culture is not something defined on paper, it's what is projected as the organizational theme. The professionalism projected within the department and in the community. Culture is a concept. It encompasses the social behavior, institutions, and norms found in society, as well as the knowledge, beliefs, arts, laws, customs, capabilities, and habits of the individuals in these groups. Culture often originated from or attributed to a specific region or location.

What was achieved in NYC from the inception of SQF in 1993 was the atmosphere of unity. A surge in broken windows policing returned NYC to a vibrant, safe city. And through natural evolution and attrition the NYPD transitioned into the most diverse police department in the nation. The main goal of crime reduction was achieved. The organizational culture blossomed, reflecting the diversity of the department.

NYPD espoused pride. Pride in their appearance, the way they carried themselves, their conduct, and the respect they projected to the community. Without sacrificing the use of positive police tactics (SQF), the police controlled the streets, not the "perps." Having only one function… to enforce the law. Not reforming the justice system, not playing social worker, and not making arrests based on racial equity. That was the organizational culture of the NYPD.

This culture of enforcement was evident between 1993 and 1997. In NYC a forty-four percent drop in felonies. A sixty percent drop in homicides and non-negligent homicides. A forty-six percent drop in burglaries, and a forty-eight percent drop in robberies and property crime. Between 1993 and 1999 overall crime declined by fifty percent. NYC led the nation in crime reduction and a culture that continued to cultivate a positive enforcement platform through a diverse team of officers. And not just NYC, crime dropped across the nation during the 1990s. This became a phenomenon coined "The Greatest American Crime Decline."

The foundational question must be asked; was SQF inherent to a racist NYPD and other urban police departments? Or was that a vague perception? Let's examine. In 1994, was the NYPD a diverse department racially balanced to the population of the communities they served? No. In 1994 the racial balance of officers in the NYPD was still predominantly white, and eighty percent of NYPD leadership above the rank of Captain were white. But in the rank and file the racial disparity between the white and minority officers (Black and Latino) was only eleven percent. The department, even in 1994, was the most diverse department in the nation..

The contention of racial enforcement is contradicted not only by the change in the racial and ethnic makeup of the department, but the requirements of diversity training in command education and in service training. Regardless of contentions of racial bias, they were unfounded, political rhetoric. And the unbiased Marron Institute report validating the police enforced the law equally, across the races.

When did the culture dramatically change? In 2020, with the political firestorm of *defund the police*. The scales tipping, police vilified. The nation in an uproar. A desire to address police tactics as fascist stormtroopers! Redirecting funds from the police to support social programs and using social workers to respond to calls for service for emotional disturbed persons (EDP's). In essence as unarmed untrained first responders. What could go wrong? A poor... no commonsense decision.

"Soft on Crime" policies impacting police officers' ability to keep streets safe. The inability to execute their oaths of office to protect and serve. Zero tolerance laws; loitering, drinking in public, street prostitution removed from the books. The public ruthlessly assaulted, openly defecating and urinating on the street. Open air drug markets with used needles everywhere. A sewer of humanity. Officers unable to enforce "hands off policies" restricting officers from keeping citizens safe.

Today regardless of the natural trend of departmental diversity, social media... the all-knowing always truthful platform, has demonized the police as racist and mistrusted. Tarnished by media misinformation and political race baiting. But one thing remains crystal clear; the goal remains Community policing. Which happens every day far from the limelight. Fighting an uphill battle from the media, and social activists. These brave men and women, unbiased and color blind... policing 101.

The police adjust their operational interaction in the community with understanding and empathy. And under the new reactive practice of "respond and report", communities, primarily the black community are more subject to "home bred" thugs. Only a decade ago, it wasn't this way, and in the galaxy of New York City, far far away, the Jedi's of the NYPD, defeated the empire... members of the community and political leadership unified to curb violent crime. The force was broken windows and Stop Question and Frisk.

The reality… facts and statistics. Stop and Frisk was a bold political decision to interject transformational change! An effective police strategy to reduce gun violence by temporarily stopping citizens believed to be carrying weapons based on reasonable suspicion, not probable cause. This robust tactic effectively brought the war on illegal guns to the streets. And in no other city in the nation was this policy energized by a unity of effort from the police, public administrators, and community. NYC led the way to return the city to the people.

Checks and Balances

And the police do police themselves. NYC supports the public with an independent mechanism to ensure transparency of police officer conduct. The Civilian Complaint Review Board, or commonly known as the CCRB. Its mission:

- To encourage members of the community to file complaints when they believe they have been victims of police misconduct.
- To respect the rights of civilians and officers.
- To encourage all parties involved in a complaint to come forward and present evidence.
- To expeditiously investigate each allegation thoroughly and impartially.
- To make fair and objective determinations on the merits of each case.
- To offer civilians and officers the opportunity to mediate their complaints, when appropriate, to promote understanding between officers and the communities they serve.
- To recommend disciplinary actions that are measured and appropriate when the investigative findings substantiate that misconduct occurred.
- To engage in community outreach to educate the public about the Agency and respond to concerns relevant to the Agency's mandate.
- To report relevant issues and policy matters to the Police Commissioner and the public; and.
- To advocate for policy changes related to police oversight, transparency, and accountability that will strengthen public trust and improve police-community relations. NYC Civilian Complaint Review Board – www.nyc.gov/ccrb

An analysis of citizen grievances of SQF encounters from seventy-four precincts filed with the Civilian Complaint Review Board (CCRB) in NYC was performed from 2007 to 2013. The findings revealed that there was no coercion or repercussions against individuals filing complaints. The numbers varied by precinct, and following SQF trends, the higher numbers of complaints were filed from individuals from predominantly minority precincts. The study also noted a trend in the reasons complaints were filed, concluding that stops resulted in feelings of unfairness and procedural injustice, not a violation of law (unlawful arrests, violation of the fourth or fourteenth amendments). Transparency[46].

The primary goal in any mutual community/police relationship is to build trust. Paramount is fair and equitable policing. And it goes both ways. The first step in achieving this relationship is the police, who shoulder the responsibility to create the groundwork. Officers achieve this community bond by performing their duties respectfully, responsibly, and with the fair

---

[46] Trunc Stat Report 20131211.pdf (nyc.gov)

enforcement needed to maintain public safety. The second is the community accepting the police as their partner, joining forces to combat crime, through community – police communications. Communications the glue of community policing.

Most underserved minority communities suffer from the same broken socio-economic issues. Plagued with gun violence, drugs, failed schools, single parent households, despair, and poverty. And the number one issue that has been identified as the key element influencing children to cross the line into criminality… a culture of single-family households. Fatherless homes. A cultural issue that needs to be addressed in the community by the community. The stability of the underserved community requires self-policing. If the community demands change, there will be change. If not, the decades of long depressed socio-economic conditions will remain the acceptable norm. Regardless of sociological "theory", the transition from years of neglect will be needed to tip the scales for a return of a stable, productive community. Politicians, having their feet held to fire for campaign promises.

The police are an external catalyst. They are guests in the community. Their presence in the community is really by invitation. The community determines if the invitation will be welcoming, or if their presence will be as party crashers. That's the work of the police and community. To try and come together, to cement a bond so that even an unwelcomed invitation does not create a "Us" against "Them" adversarial relationship.

But today the organizational culture of the police is a culture of defeat. Cultural insecurity. Police attacked by a country divided along racial boundaries. Used by politicians as political pawns. The cultural plague of *Defund the Police* and *Sanctuary Cities*. Violent crime that drove the crack cocaine epidemic of the 1980s repeating itself on steroids with the influx of fentanyl. Transported across an open border by unvetted illegal aliens, criminals. Politicians sleeping at the wheel. Traffickers disappearing into the interior of the U.S. Politicians the real enemy… demonizing the police. Their ideological policies are abject failures.

The negative culture of law enforcement is so drastic, that law enforcement is teetering on their inability to protect citizens. Local departments at the breaking point. Unable to recruit, lowering standards, demoralized. Reduced to non-violent crimes being handled by artificial intelligence. Only responding to life and limb calls for service. Since 2020 the media has portrayed the police as racist, overzealous and brutal, … public scapegoats. Demands for racial equity, criminal justice reforms, alternative jail sentences, and the elimination of enforcing quality of life crimes (zero tolerance) have decimated most of our urban cities.

Plus, the legalization of marijuana and in Oregon… hard drugs. Creating a "free for all" of crime. In the 1980s petty criminals ruled the streets of New York… squeegee degenerates, graffiti painters, prostitutes, and drug dealers. In 2025 cities were burdened by homeless encampments, zero enforcement of quality-of-life crimes. The influx of illegals, and their criminal element. Illegal gangs, like the notorious Tren De Agua terrorize communities. Of course, their reins of terror openly covered up in sanctuary cities. Welcoming these "new arrivals." Now illegals are being protected, radical left-wing Governors and Mayors promising to protect them from ICE, in direct violation of federal statutes. While doing nothing to protect US citizens. And gun violence rampant, in our urban cities, being committed by US citizens, violent thugs, many set back on the street under *no cash bail*. Citizens lives in peril, afraid to walk the streets. Political rhetoric to pass more gun legislation. But what is being done to protect residents in NYC, Washington, D.C., Chicago, New Orleans, Seattle, and other self-created sanctuary cities? Apparently, criminals have a free pass. Public safety, once the number one priority of government, secondary to political pandering and radical left ideology.

The police culture… survive. A national mass exodus of seasoned, experienced officers. In the NYPD retirement has jumped to record numbers. The chart below demonstrates the trend of officers' retirements in the NYPD from 2020 to 2023. Urban departments follow suit.

Year	Numbers	Percentage Increase
2020	1092	--
2022	1596	38%
2023	2516	43%

Table 5 - NYPD Retirement Trends

The same trend of cultural demoralization has affected those cities that jumped on the band wagon to *Defund the Police*. Each city has transformed from a once elegant cultural vestige to cesspools of out-of-control crime, homelessness, and an invasion of illegal migrants.

Policing once considered an honorable profession… now a pariah. A political sacrificial lamb. Attacked daily by the far-left media. The hypocrisy is absurd. Law enforcement will always remain the first line of defense against crime. And when the haters, the woke, call, the police will respond, expected to shoulder the mantel of responsibility to protect and serve. Even with their hands tied behind their backs. And they will run to the sound of danger, then be chastised for doing their jobs. Solid police enforcement, the new concept imploding. The experiment of eliminating standards, racial diversity, equity, and inclusion in policing has failed. Can the country recover from political indifference? How long will it take? In New Orleans January 1, 2025, an act of terrorism killed ten citizens. Driving into a crowd on a street that was supposed to have been cordoned off by barriers. Who was in charge, who did the threat assessments, where were cops? A DEI sanctuary city, with a police department and Mayor identified as one of the top three corrupt departments and Mayors in the nation. Result… blood on their hands… no one held accountable. Change… zero..

The political solution to cook the books to reflect acceptable statistics. How… for one… reduce felonies to misdemeanors. Second, track certain crimes, not as crimes, the shell game. Assaults by emotionally disturbed persons, not categorized as a felony assault, tracked as a mental health event. Inaccurate reporting. And since 2021 many departments across the nation have not reported crime statistics in the NIBRS (National Incident Based Reporting System)[47]. And to solve the staffing problem several states; California, and Illinois have introduced legislation to allow non-citizens to become police officers. New York, Maryland, and D.C. are

---

[47] National Incident-Based Reporting System (NIBRS) | Bureau of Justice Statistics (ojp.gov)

also considering this legislation. Non-citizens would be empowered to enforce the laws of the land. Los Angeles has already initiated this policy. Never in our nation's history have we embraced the "inclusion" of "mercenaries." to enforce US constitutional law. The push by politicians to pursue socialism, using fascist tactics... the new political Storm Troopers.

Unfortunately, the generation of new officers has a culture based on a two-inch screen and thumb magic of texting. Reliance on social media. In the street, observation is the difference in life and death. Perps, terrorists, could have just walked past them, committed a crime and been on their way. Departments reduced physical and appearance standards. Overweight officers, beards, and ponytails. And the NYPD along with other departments allow waivers for certain misdemeanors. How do you maintain police legitimacy?.

Hmm... if there is a chemical attack, how does an officer seat their protective mask on their face with facial hair... they don't... casualty. Overweight officers, how do I rely on them in a foot chase... I can't. My life placed in danger. Ponytails are the best. A threat stalks a female or male officer, the officer is on their phone (normal) the assailant grabs ponytail from behind... has total control of the officer. Pulls out a knife and while pulling the officer off balance, reaches around and stabs the officer in the chest or in the throat. Playing this game will get officers killed.

Who bears the brunt of officers reduced standards... the public. Quality and professionalism disappear with the changing political climate. Officers on patrol focused on their iPhone, not aggressively looking for individuals or maintaining situational awareness. Setting themselves up to be targets. The new generation Millennials and Gen Z lost in the cyber cloud. Another challenge for incoming officers... lack of interpersonal communications skills. Causing a problem in their ability to interact with the public. The "old breed" cop relied on personnel communications skills and face to face interaction to get the job done. Taught in the academy... verbal judo. The practice enabled officers, the "beat cops" to use dialogue to engage the community, establish relationships, build trust and through this partnership, gain intelligence. Using verbal judo as a principal police tool to diffuse situations. And it worked. Because of "verbal judo" and conversational interaction with the community, how many crimes were averted, the numbers are immeasurable. Communication is still a critical tool in policing. Part of the art of common-sense policing..

Now the phrase... "de-escalation" the new "modern" police, media, and political lexicon. Verbal judo is not politically correct. But the concept is the same. Unfortunately, the days of the beat cops are no more. Now officers respond to calls for service in patrol cars. They respond, report, and depart. Removed from the community, part time visitors. The unwelcome visitors of Community Policing. Revolving in mainly minority communities. The community aware of police inability to police their neighborhoods due to staffing shortages. No cash bail and soft on crime policies will have criminals back on the street in hours. And the cops feel abandoned... and they are. The strained trust between the community and police has been eroded. The rubber band stretched so thin it's ready to snap..

Chapter 13 – Urban Decay – Public Perception

For many departments, including NYC, Chicago, New Orleans, Washington, D.C., violent crime has soared. Regardless of how crime statistics have been politically manipulated. And in 2025, every crime ridden city statistically has miraculously reported major drops in index crimes The community and political demographic are a critical point of interest. Each urban area affected by out-of-control crime is governed by a minority mayor, minority city council and a black Chief of Police. Is there a direct correlation to minority controlled urban cities violent crime? Plenty of political rhetoric of how crime must be mitigated… yet no innovative policing strategies that have contributed to reducing crime. The tally of deaths of innocent civilians continues to rise. And politicians… don't even blink an eye. Ignorance is bliss. And there is plenty of ignorance to go around.

And the media helps cover up the incompetence. They are the shield to protect the guilty politicians who perpetuated violence with their chants of defund the police. And unfortunately, the criminal profile in each community has not deviated in decades: young black juveniles in minority communities. The FBI annual Uniformed Crime Report for the past five years (2019-2023) reporting the domestic threat to urban communities remains black on black crime. With no end in sight. Let's recap:

A. NYC reported three hundred eighty homicides in 2023, down by eleven percent from 2022. However, NYC remains unsafe with violent assaults being committed on the transit system (subways), in open public, by young black perps and violent gangs of illegals. Perpetrators released under New York State's ludicrous *no cash bail* law. Mayor Adams and his anti-police city council and administration do nothing but rant and use their positions as anti-police platforms.

B. Chicago attained the distinction of being the "Murder Capitol of the Country" in 2023 with six hundred twenty-three homicides. Homicides in Chicago were committed twenty times higher in Black communities that in the rest of the nation. The percentage of homicides, ninety-seven percent Black on Black. Mayor Johnson totally ignoring the plight of the Black community, diverting funds to support programs for illegal migrant.

C. Washington, D.C. in 2023 with two hundred seventy-four homicides. The highest murder rate since 1997. D.C. violent crime, one hundred percent Black on Black. The perpetrators were as young as eleven. The victims… children, elderly men and women, innocent citizens. Total disregard for life. The solution, the DEI -*Woke* Police Chief and Mayor holding meetings and safety walks. Single and multiple shootings a daily occurrence. Schools in the district are plagued with violence. In 2025 reduced homicides, but currently the numbers of shootings and vicious assaults is on track to break another record for violent crime. Not so says Mayor Bowser. And the effectiveness on reducing crime with useless rhetoric – ZERO.

The public is left in a quandary. Public perception is convoluted by inaction. What has suffered is the public's perception of police legitimacy. Citizens begging for safe communities. The theoretical goal - fair interaction between the police and community. Unfortunately, under today's police landscape, the community only see officers after the shootings… during the crime scene investigation. The current climate in urban cities is less than favorable. Members of the community are prisoners in their own homes. The Ferguson effect, fear of scrutinization and prosecution. It's the fact that officers are stretched to the limit. Short staffed, mandatory overtime, teetering on exhaustion. What will happen in 2025… hope, faith that the police will be given the authority to "Protect and Serve." And it appears it finally has.

Balancing Police Strategies and Public Opinion

There are two fundamental sides of the controversy regarding SQF. Those who view SQF as an effective police tool that is effective as an active police procedure and deterrent to control and reduce crime. The result… safer communities. The other opinion, an unfair police tactic that is discriminatory, targeting minorities. Politicians searching for the elusive "systemic root cause." The pot stirred and fueled by a bias politically driven media.

The Ferguson riots in August of 2014, the death of Eric Garner in July 2014, and the tumultuous national outcry of the death of George Floyd in May 2020, raised the outcry of defund the police. Police brutality, racist police tactics, became the number one issue in the country. The media crucified the administration and the police. Enforcing the law in a minority community… taboo. A wedge dividing the nation. Well, here we are in 2025. Under the Biden -Harris administration, the nation was force-fed DEI and woke policies. Law enforcement caught in its vice. Policing by diversity equity and inclusion. The question… what improvements have been made by the ideological policies?

The same picture comes into view. Ferguson remains one of the most dangerous communities in the United States. Minneapolis, where George Floyd was killed, has a violent crime rate of twenty-three percent, twice as high as the national average. St. Louis only a few miles away from Ferguson rated number one in the nation for violent crime. And it's not only the innocent civilians that are in the line of fire. Policies that allow violent criminals back onto the community within hours. A national crime survey was conducted in November 2024. The country declared that we're moving in the wrong direction. Yet the country remains divided. There are still jurisdictions that will continue to enforce soft on crime policies. How that will be dealt with… stay tuned.

The term procedural justice identifies community encounters with officers. Based on these encounters, the community determines their opinions of police practices (enforcement). Are they just or unjust, will they be obeyed? How would the underrepresented urban communities assess procedural justice today? I would make a bold assumption that urban communities see procedural justice as injustice. The sad situation is that many urban politicians have ignored or replaced the needs of the community for their own personal and political agenda. They don't care about their constituents. Unless they are campaigning for re-election or need media coverage.

The difference between procedural justice during the SQF era and now. The government was pro-active in reducing crime, regardless of the racial overtones. Policies and funds were directed to reduce violent crime. SQF was controversial, no doubt, but the results were making a difference to Public Safety. Public Perception was uncontested. Societal impacts to provide safety for every community were being achieved. More importantly the mental outlook of citizens of all colors and ethnicities was positive… they felt safe.

Building trust is paramount in fair and equitable policing. It goes both ways. Regardless of the two-way street, it falls on the shoulders of the officers to set the groundwork to attain the community's trust and respect. Officers achieve this community bond by performing their duties respectfully, responsibly, and with the fair balance to accomplish the procedural justice needed to maintain public safety. The community has faith and believes that the police will be honest and fair. Yet only when both sides can come together, can there be fair and equitable procedural justice.

The police are an external catalyst. They are guests in the community. Their presence in the community is really by invitation. The community determines if the invitation will be at the behest of the community or considered uninvited. That's the work of the police and community. To try and come together in a bond so that even an unwelcome invitation does not pit "Us" against "Them." Can that even happen today?

It's a challenge that remains elusive in most underserved minority communities. For decades they have suffered from the same broken socio-economic issues. Plagued with gun violence, drugs, failed schools, single parent households, despair, and poverty. And the number one issue that has been identified as the key element influencing children to cross the line into criminality… single-family households. Fatherless homes. A cultural issue that needs to be addressed in the community by the community. The stability of the community requires self-policing by the community. If the community demands change, there will be change. If not, the decades long socio-economic conditions, poverty will continue to plague these communities… remaining the acceptable norm.

Chapter 14 – Public Education – A Playground for Crime

We must evaluate the external influences that are contributing to our youth becoming statistics of violent crime. One of those is the glaring failure of the public education system. Educators, in underrepresented communities, have lost control. School shootings, unprovoked attacks on children by children. "Students," many willing participants, cheer on the violence. An acceptable daily occurrence in our nation's urban and rural public schools.

Educating children preparing them to be productive members of society has been replaced with drag shows, indoctrination to critical race theory, transgender boys being permitted to use girl's bathrooms and locker rooms. Assaults on school busses, drugs use in schools ignored and sexual assaults, in many schools, Loudon County, Virgina, covered up. Schools have become the basic training grounds for future criminals. School administrators with their heads in the "cloud." Eliminating school resource officers but ensuring NARCAN is available for students if they overdose on fentanyl. Reporting overdoses to parent…?

But what about the atrocious test scores? Teaching critical race theory in underrepresented schools, indoctrinating young black students that they are oppressed… denying students encouragement, pigeonholing them. Stressing that their race and ethnicity will determine their station in life. Too many ending up committing crimes. We heard this in 1930s Europe. Same play book.

No concern for their emotional health. Education should be a concept of opportunity. It should be a constitutional right of every student, without prejudice. Provide the foundation to teach a viable curriculum. Not spew social justice. Teach the subject, afford every student the opportunity to succeed and help identify those students that struggle and provide the help necessary. With the realization, every student has special qualities. Some academically inclined. Some with an aptitude for the trades. Everyone does not possess the same talents. The job of the educators is to identify, mentor and help students pursue a career according to aptitude… not inhibit the capabilities putting them in an equity pigeonhole.

Worse, pandering educators with their PhD's, in their suits stating and re-stating the same excuses. Making false promises how they are going to address the educational deficiencies. Administrators contributing to the demise. Students not held accountable. Teaching students that it's OK to act out, moving on past the broken window. Forget zero tolerance… zero consequences.

Attempting to use mediation as the tool to curb students who have demonstrated unacceptable repeat behaviors, committing assaults, harassment, and bullying. Failing to accept the fact that if students are acting out, and failing in school, the problem extends well beyond the school campus. A problem exists in the home. Which is a revolving door problem in a vast number of underrepresented public schools. With the problem directly related to the number one problem in minority households … the absence of fathers.

In many school districts, what was once a hallowed tradition... high school football has become a platform for gang violence and shootings. Violent behavior in the stands a normal evening out. Metal detectors require parents and students to be searched for weapons. Parents acting out... committing assaults. Their violent behavior mirrored by their children on the field. What type of example is being set by the parents? And bad behavior begetting bad behavior. Shootings part of the half time and post-game show. The game cheer... screams of fear.

School violence jumped to almost forty-five percent in 2023[48]. School campuses are becoming a societal hub of youth crime. Not a public education problem, a public safety problem. Educators continue to identify charts and paper strategies that have no impact or influence on providing a safe and secure educational environment. Not qualified to deal with school violence, they have failed in their responsibility to protect their students. And if teachers intervene in a physical altercation... threatened with termination. And the reason for the teacher intervention is irrelevant. Whether to protect a student from bodily harm or from unwanted advances. The teacher is wrong, facing disciplinary action to include termination. Who's in charge of the zoo? And many schools are a menagerie. All verifiable.

The truancy rate for underrepresented communities is languishing at forty percent.[49] Where are the parents in the educational equation? You can't expect to hold students accountable when responsibility and life skills are not being learned at home. If parents are disinterested in their children, they will switch schools. They'll attend the school of the "Streets." They'll become A students in assault, robbery, and may graduate to drive by shootings, carjackings and homicide.

What happens to these underrepresented students who the education system fails? They become rolled up in a power point statistic. An astounding five percent end up in the juvenile system.[50] Precipitated by lack of parents parenting, kids turning to social media and the street to receive their education. Where is the outcry to dismantle the politically controlled education unions? The one that is paid to represent the teachers and discard the students. Protected by political elites.

Educators' priorities. Proper pronouns, transgender equity, using bathrooms of your desired gender. Ensuring every student regardless of their parent's objection or religious belief encouraged and supported to transition should they choose. Social equity, attempting to remove the legal rights of the parents. Assisting in illegally overstepping parents legal rights? That is educational tyranny.

PhD's who tinker with the lives of students as a social experiment, with radical educational agendas. So removed from the conditions minority students deal with when they leave the confines of the school. For many their only solace. A place to receive a decent meal, a haven. Mentally and physically.

---

[48] District of Columbia Attendance Report 2022-23 School Year November 30, 2023
[49] District of Columbia Attendance Report 2022-23 School Year November 30, 2023
[50] POLICY BRIEF Youth Justice by the Numbers by Joshua Rovner   August 14, 2024

The unvarnished truth… failed parental involvement, lack of counseling, minimal to zero discipline and accountability. And the ridiculous law that allows keeping disruptive students in school until they reach the age of majority (twenty-one)[51]. New York State failed "tactics" that entices continued bad behavior, without fear of consequence. Training grounds for seventy percent of the next generation of criminals. And that's fact.

Where is the outcry to dismantle the politically controlled education system? The United Federation of Teachers, nothing more than a political party, pushing their agenda. Their dues paying members and political network all benefit from keeping kids in failed public schools. Numbers and statistics equal federal aid and a bargaining chip in educational policy, teacher salaries and benefit packages. The public education solution… lowering and eliminating standardized test scores. The work around to hide students lacking basic education. NYC, Chicago and Montgomery County, Maryland, have gone to "performance assessments." Subjective assessments. Allowing the teacher to perform an assessment, not on the student's capability, but to ensure that they cover their ass. Failing a student is not reflective on the student's learning ability, but in the eyes of the union, reflects on the teachers. Social advancement… move kids through the system. I wonder where these caring educators think these kids will end up.

Removing school resource officers? The numbers of school shootings since 2020 have not subsided, in fact has increased. Liberals who have demanded police school resource officers (SRO) be removed from schools, with the insanity that they pose a threat to minority children, are ideological hypocrites. No where near the classroom. The National Center for Educational Statistics - July 2024 report is staggering. In 2020–21, there were a total of forty-one school-associated violent deaths in the United States, which included twenty homicides and seventeen suicides.

Of these forty-one school-associated violent deaths, eleven homicides and six suicides were of school-age youth (ages five–eighteen). From 2000 through 2022, there were three hundred twenty-eight casualties (one hundred thirty-one killed and one hundred ninety-seven wounded) in active shooter incidents at elementary and secondary schools and one hundred fifty-seven casualties (seventy-five killed and eighty-two wounded) in active shooter incidents at postsecondary institutions.[52]

School Resource Officers have a negative impact on students, especially students of color? Ideological pandering. Another social experiment that places the lives of students in jeopardy. As of July 2020, the Center reported that school shootings have increased by one hundred twenty-four percent. Yet when there is a school shooting, who runs to the sound of the threat to protect the students? The police (SROs).

Political pandering of school unions creating roadblocks for alternate school choice. A path for success. Organized, students held accountable, enforced discipline and social skills. Not what the teachers' unions want. Fighting to keep public schools off balance. Pursuing a

---

[51] New York Bill Passed Extending Time for Students with IEPs To Complete Schooling (accessibility.com)
[52] COE - Violent Deaths at School and Away from School, and Active Shooter Incidents (ed.gov)

communist manifesto of total control, eliminating parental authority. Keeping underrepresented students' prisoner in a system that has failed them for decades.

We have played the game of appeasement too long. Not all kids will be academic geniuses. A progressive visionary, President Roosevelt in 1933 created the Civilian Conservation Corps (CCC).[53] Roosevelt creating an opportunity for those suffering from unemployment from the great depression, building a national work force to rebuild our nation's infrastructure. It was successful. Put at-risk kids to work. Forced labor... hardly. Take them out of the failed counter-productive educational environments. Give them pride in workmanship. Teach them a trade. Let them rebuild our infrastructure. Teach them the meaning of a good day's work. Yes, under a semi-military environment, holding them accountable, instilling self-worth and pride. Allowing them to have a chance to succeed. Many of these young men and women only know the "horrors of urban warfare."

Do it on a large scale. While there is the federal Job Corps, that program is sparse and only scratches the surface of numbers of underrepresented young men and women who need structure and a chance to change their lives Unless bold and drastic actions are taken, underrepresented primarily black youth will remain the forgotten class, destined to remain not in the circle of life, but the circle of desperation, crime and incarceration.

---

[53] Civilian Conservation Corps (CCC) (u-s-history.com)

Chapter 15 – Measures of Success or Failure

This chapter provides minority NYC police officers' perception of the success of SQF. The results offer a greater insight from this unique group of officers. Is their definition of success the same as police administrators? Is it the same as members of the minority community? No, but their perceptions are honest and upfront, not restricted by politics or police bureaucracy. What were their perceptions of how supervisors, the department and administration measured success in reducing gun violence? Captured in this chapter are the human aspects of emotions, frustrations and concerns of minority officers who executed SQF. This chapter provides their story as they went about the daily task of maintaining public safety in NYC.

Measurements of success are commonly based on statistical methods. But that is only one of a litany of variables that measure success or failure. And during the SQF era it was the *only* reliable source used by the NYPD to measure SQF success. Why is this perspective so important? Because they were bypassed by city leadership… their voices ignored. CompStat the single measure of success. Lacking the key element of the human factor… feedback from the field. This approach intentionally tipped the scales of success in favor of the police and city administration.

Statistics don't include the inter-personal relationships between the police and the community. The pain felt from the loss of a child or a family member. And for the police… a fallen officer. Anger and frustration from daily indiscriminate gun violence. And the wedge of the community more afraid of being stopped by the police to meet the UF 250's quota, than from the gun violence plaguing the community. A new term arising from the black community… Walking While Black.[54] Fear of being stopped by the police for the crime of being black (regardless the race of the police officer).

The full court press at the beginning of SQF (1994) included all the key stakeholders; police executives, mayor's office, community groups, police officers, and opinions from citizens would have been the correct measurement equation. But SQF became a political football… unity dissolved. Battle lines were drawn. Supporters and challengers. More like a heavy weight boxing match. The police in one corner, and the NYC ACLU in the other. Twisting the numbers, manipulating the same statistics to make their argument, pro or con. A statistical quandary. Police officer's input from their extensive experience in the street kept in the precincts.

A comparative study found that SQF led to the seizure of seven hundred eighty-nine firearms during 2011. However, SQF encounters in 2011 totaled more than six hundred eighty-five thousand. Weapons seizure occurred in less than one percent per eight hundred SQF events. These findings are consistent with studies that suggested the stops measured from 2007 to 2013, were not only disproportionate by population but also counterproductive. Or did it show that SQF not only achieved its goal but was a success as a deterrent. Or did it

---

[54] Walking While Black — ProPublica

demonstrate success and the need for a program review and recasting of resources. Still an effective police tool in reducing gun violence. Success or failure… which side do you believe was fair and honest?

When SQF became a political football, and political lines drawn, success or failure no longer mattered. The people of the city of New York didn't matter. What mattered was pandering and jockeying for position. The intended goal, … to take guns off the streets became secondary. The NYPD measure of success was void of politics. It was simple, derived from a standard formula: numbers of stops equal productivity of reduced index crimes equal program success. The same formula was used in reverse by the ACLU: numbers of stops equal disproportionate stops of blacks equals minimal effectiveness in taking guns off the street. Two perspectives using the same numbers. Political influence and external pressure. Clouded perceptions, media sensationalism, and political pandering to communities of color were the driving force behind the demise of SQF.

What represents the actual model of success or failure? Not CompStat and not numbers and statistics. The true model … the community model. Built by the stakeholders and executed fairly and honestly. Building a trilogy of trust and accountability. With measurable and achievable short- and long-term socio-economic goals. That means admitting failure, accepting responsibility, taking a hard deep dive to identify and eliminate distractors. However, the scourge of political divisiveness, especially in this *defund the police* era, nothing is achieved. No one admits their mistakes. Everyone circles their wagons, divided along political ideology.

The political strategy… blame the other party. Lie and then lie again. A shell game. Avoiding the truth at all costs. Are the wounds from the political sword gutting the minority communities ever going to heal? God knows, but the shame, whose sacrificing community safety. Leading the charge of *defund the police* and *no cash bail* are minority politicians. Using these communities as pawns for re-election. The revolving door. Is there a chance that disadvantaged communities will ever achieve socio-economic independence? Is it a bridge too far.

Yes, statistics reflect a reduction of gun violence in urban cities across the nation. Politicians and the media running like chickens with their heads cut off professing this great accomplishment. I contend that this is no more than a cover up, a conspiracy. Hard to see how crime is down, while shootings continue to take the lives of innocent people in underrepresented communities. And in our most violent cities, Washington, D.C., NYC, Baltimore, Chicago, St. Louis, Milwaukie "statistics" do not provide a metric of success or failure to a parent who has just lost a child from indiscriminate gun violence. Statistics do not provide bullet proofing to keep people from getting shot! .

One thing that is uncontested by statistics is the demographics where violent crime continues out of control. Where is the emphasis to eradicate those offenders who plague those communities, like locusts? Lock them up and hold them accountable? Where is the emphasis to ensure tranquility and security in the low-income minority communities? These communities remain no more than a checkerboard for politicians.

During the twenty years of the SQF era the goal to reduce index crimes to a sustainable level was achieved. But without policy review, developing a political life of its own. Widening the gap of community mistrust and creating fear of the police. This drives a conclusion that policies need to be evaluated at scheduled intervals. Common sense prevails… to assure efficiencies of public value and stewardship of appropriations. What is at stake… can SQF and zero tolerance be reintroduced as a societal model to reduce crime?

Statistics do not represent the feelings and opinions of individuals and groups. The only true measure of success from a program or political perspective is its public value. Is SQF past, present and future a program that protects the community and saves lives? And the glaring void; officers as a variable in the measurement equation. The quotes below provides the opinions of those officers who were interviewed. The debate continues.

The community of common sense was silenced after the Floyd killing in May of 2020. The political outcry blamed the police, all police of being the racist gestapo. Race and identity politics the new framework of equity policing. The country surrendered to the quagmire of political insanity. The safety and security of citizens placed on the back burner. The new measure of success… the barometer of public opinion. A revolution demanding social equity.

Officer Quotes

"I think stop, question, and frisk was effective. Was it always utilized in the right way? No. But there are good and bad in everything. There's always… the right thing for the wrong reasons."

"When it's used properly, it's an outstanding tool… into the garbage pail; it sullies the efforts of a good stop. It undermines the efforts of the police department."

"It was like an open season. I think it started with good intentions, trying to deter crime… how that commanding officer determined what he had to do, especially when it comes to CompStat."

"Did we cross the line in terms of people's liberties and civil liberties and stuff? Yes, I guess. But you know what… I just got a gun off the streets that was going to kill my cousin or my nephew, right?"

"What happened was, it became a numbers game. Because of CompStat. If you use it the way it was meant to be used, the way it was intended, it absolutely works."

"The shift, part of the shift came from; people felt safer against crime, saying, "I fear the police (more) stopping my son."

"Of course, there's no crime, but people should be a whole lot safer. As a matter of fact, I can't even say that the people felt a whole lot safer."

"Most people want to live in a safe place, a safe environment… addressing that issue was demanded by all sides."

"If I did something five times and it yielded nothing, I'm going to start… out to be nothing."

"I need to scale back so that I'm not stopping so many people for no reason."

Chapter 16 – Policing Strategies

Police strategies to ensure the safety and security were effective until 2020. Now enforcement strategies have been prohibited by judicial parameters. Now those strategies have been reversed. Generic strategies, such as adding more officers to a department, random patrolling, rapid response to calls, and arrest procedures are archaic. Politicians believing that social workers should replace uniformed officers to deal with non-life-threatening calls for service for the mentally ill and emotionally disturbed persons. What is not understood… every call has the potential of being dangerous. Replacing common sense with ideology policing.

What strategies are effective? Community policing, hot spot tactics and problem-oriented policing. The strategies of the Stop Question and Frisk era. Today's strategies in the anti-police – *defund the police* era… *no cash bail*. Defeating effective policing. Opening the flood gates, putting criminals back on the street as quickly as they can be processed and released. Citizens living in fear.

In the 1990s, NYC Police Commissioner Bratton with the support from the mayor introduced two initiatives to reduce crime; "Reclaiming the Public Spaces of New York" and "Getting Guns off the Streets of New York." Grounded in traditional policing methods, founded in broken windows. Establishing forceful campaigns to arrest and jail low level and petty criminals. Strengthening the authority of the officers to approach individuals behaving inappropriately. The introduction of Zero Tolerance and Stop Question and Frisk. The result… safer communities, safer citizens. The public… enthusiastic. The stress of being a victim of crime is significantly reduced.

Street Crimes Unit (SCU)

Bratton also introduced a specialized unit, the street crimes unit (SCU). Assisting in hot spot zero tolerance policing, but their main effort, gun suppression. From 1971 to 1997, the unit was made up of sixty to one hundred officers. In 2000 it expanded to three hundred members. It employed innovative methods, including the earliest coordinated sting operations to arrest elicit potential muggers. According to *Criminal Justice Today*: "The SCU disguised officers as potential mugging victims and put them in areas where they were most likely to be attacked." The SCU would go into high-crime neighborhoods and make a much larger number of firearms-related arrests in comparison to uniformed patrol officers.

In 1973, the SCU won recognition as an Exemplary Project from the U.S. Law Enforcement Assistance Administration (LEAA). LEAA was the United States' leading crime-reduction and crime-prevention funding agency. "In its first year, the SCU made nearly four thousand arrests and averaged a successful conviction rate of around eighty percent. The most telling statistic was the average officer day per arrest." The SCU invested eight days in each arrest, whereas the department average for all uniformed officers was one hundred fifty-seven days.[55]

---

[55] NEW YORK CITY POLICE DEPARTMENT STREET CRIME UNIT - AN EXEMPLARY PROJECT | Office of Justice Programs (ojp.gov)

According to the U.S. Commission for Civil Rights, SCU filed "twenty-seven thousand stop and frisk reports" in 1998.[56] The greatest number generated by any NYPD unit. In April 1999, the subjects of all stop and frisk reports registered by the SCU were sixty-four percent black, twenty percent Hispanic, six percent white, and one-half percent Asian. Consistent with CompStat. SCU's increased enforcement was not without repercussions. Numerous harassment complaints revealing that twenty-three percent of stops were outside the rules regarding reasonable suspicion. SCU coming under national scrutiny and outrage in the aftermath of the shooting of an unarmed African immigrant, Amadou Diallo in the Bronx in February 1999. The elite SCU division dissolved in 2002 following a federal investigation and several highly visible media events, including at least one shooting, use of excessive force, sexual harassment, and deaths of suspects.

The unit was reactivated in 2015, the Strategic Response Group, with a new name - "City Wide Anti-Crime Unit." The new City-Wide Anti-Crime Unit is more investigative, and intelligence based than the former Street Crimes Unit. In 2020, anti-crime units across the city were disbanded once again following the death of George Floyd. These combined strategies were criticized due to their widespread use of the controversial disorder strategy of SQF and cry of police targeting black citizens. But one thing is crystal clear... during their existence their success was unquestioned.

Return of the Street Crimes Unit

In response to a wave of violence during his first month on the job – capped by a deadly attack on two police officers – NYC Mayor Eric Adams resurrected the controversial unit within the NYPD to help stem an increase in shootings (2022). Hoping that oversight and training will prevent the unit from the infamy that plagued it in years past. The so-called anti-crime unit, which was disbanded in August 2020 following racial justice protests and unrest across the country, rebranded ... Neighborhood Safety Teams. The unit and other similarly composed units have been marked by allegations of aggressive tactics and police brutality.[57]

Unfortunately, in the past, the history of the SCU shows that plainclothes officers were really some of the worst offenders when it came to abusive and discriminatory policing. Why? Possible lack of training or the lack of oversight and accountability to attain "the numbers." Regardless of violation of individual constitutional rights. The same concept... undercover officers integrating into the heart of thirty of the most dangerous precincts in the city. Identify violent perpetrators, affects arrests. With strict oversight and accountability of supervisors. Strictly adhering to NYPD arrest policies.

But by June 2023, the Neighborhood Safety Teams (NSTs)were being scrutinized for affecting disproportionate arrests on people of color.[58] Deja Vu? Two differences from the SCU era. Most officers on the NSTs are Black and Hispanic, reflecting the neighborhoods they

---

[56] Executive Summary (usccr.gov)

[57] The NYPD has resurrected its controversial anti-crime unit. Success will be determined by avoiding mistakes of the past | CNN

[58] NYPD safety team making high number of unlawful stops, mostly people of color: Report - ABC News (go.com)

patrol. The arrests have been validated with weapons being taken off perpetrators. Is it disproportionate enforcement, or is there a root cause why so many minorities (Blacks) are committing crimes with guns? The story of NSTs continues to evolve.

And the NSTs have helped return broken windows policing. Most recently the NYPD has generated a crackdown on low level crimes.[59] Concentrating in times square, citing illegal vendors, and taking pedicabs off the street. Enforcing Quality of Life violations. Apparently to protect the tourist industry. Something that was initiated during the Guiliani administration by Commissioner Bratton… Zero Tolerance. History repeating itself returning "what worked." With the exception that it took a decade to be re-introduced. The city returning to Common Sense policing.

However, in more democratic controlled states, crime reduction strategy continues to concentrate on strict gun control legislation discouraging citizens gun ownership. And apparently under the Biden- Harris administration a desire to strip guns from the hands of legal owners. Challenging their second amendment rights. Then the only people that will have guns will be… Criminals!

Community Intervention

Many urban cities in their crime reduction strategies have implemented amnesty programs. Cash for guns… allowing citizens to turn in guns without question or fear of prosecution. In Chicago, the Cure Violence (CV)[60] model was introduced. Previously named Chicago Ceasefire, it was a community driven effort funded and run privately. The Cure Violence effort encouraged individuals to turn in their guns, with the hope that it would have an impact on curtailing violent crime. The premise, "violence follows usual epidemiological patterns."

When you look at charts, graphs and maps, the trends in violence follows the same pattern as an epidemic. You can think of the flu, AIDS or COVID epidemic. First there are very few cases, then it spreads from one carrier infecting a community. Violence, like an epidemic is extremely contagious. The requirement for intervention becomes obvious, you must interact with the people who have been *infected*. Strategies associated with epidemic disease control: detecting and interrupting conflicts, identifying and treating the highest risk individuals, and changing social norms.

The success of intervention programs quickly transitioned into other major cities: Philadelphia, Phoenix, Pittsburgh, and Boston. Providing measurable outcomes indicating declines in violence, a reduction in shootings, and fewer homicides. From 2004 to 2012, modeling showed promising outcomes in reducing violent gun related crime.

The NYPD has a similar strategy to voluntarily allow citizens to turn in guns. Cash for Guns, an active program that pays two hundred dollars for any gun turned in. No questions asked. A program still in effect. Washington, D.C. launched "Peace for D.C." in 2021.[61] Peace for D.C.

[59] NYPD Midtown sweep targets illegal vendors, quality-of-life crimes _ FOX 5 New York

[60] Program Profile: Cure Violence (Chicago, Ill.) | CrimeSolutions, National Institute of Justice (ojp.gov)

[61] peace for dc - Search (bing.com)

brings together community-based organizations, experts, and policymakers to reduce gun violence in neighborhoods with high rates of violence. They focus on evidence-based programs, data-driven strategies, and collaboration to save lives. In NYC it's called CompStat and hot spot policing.

Three community-based programs, three initiatives, but how effective have those strategies worked... where are the statistics, have they made an impact on reducing gun violence? And yet there is the irony that buyback programs are intended to have illegal guns turned in. That law abiding citizens who have exercised second amendment rights for self-protection in urban cities have been arrested, charged with felony assault with a weapon. The scales of justice seems to be catering to criminals.

Violence Interrupters

The strategy of violence interrupters looked good on paper. But these convicted felons, and that's what they are, have done absolutely nothing to curb violence. Except for taking thousands of dollars and helping mold criminals to be better criminals. In Washington, D.C. Mayor Bowser was asked by the local news station WJLA Channel 7 what the impact of the violence interrupter program was. The D.C. tap dance... we'll get back to you. And most recently the FBI arrested a city councilmember for taking bribes, accepting cash to influence violence interrupter contracts.[62]

The D.C. program sponsored by the Office of Neighborhood Safety and Engagement (ONSE), allocated an annual budget of seven million dollars. Of course, as this predominantly black community struggles for survival, the FBI investigation has found that records tracking the program of the five vendors contracted by D.C. are incomplete or have gone missing[63]. Yet the program remains funded by the D.C. City council. No data of the impact of difference violence interrupters have made in any of the D.C. communities.

The same tap dance is being performed in NYC with their violence interrupter program. Yet they are getting paid up to one hundred thousand dollars. No accountability, money thrown to the wind. Their effect on crime reduction... known but to God. No records, just another pandering wasteful government program. In NYC, not to anyone's surprise, cops and violence interrupters do not work together as partners.

Another program fraught with waste fraud and abuse. And to top it off, Mayor Bowser has mandated, that the term convicted felon be taken out of the D. C. lexicon. Referring them as "returning citizens." Making them feel welcome as they reintegrate. The majority, more than 70% will end up committing crimes, returning to prison. Will they be welcomed back into the criminal justice system as... returning felons. This wasteful program is not tracked. Money just disappears. No more than political patronage handouts. You wonder if these contracts and their interrupters have gone through any financial or criminal background checks? What is known is that these convicted felons are no strangers to violent crime. And no one is held accountable for

---

[62] DC Council member Trayon White pleads not guilty to federal bribery charge – NBC4 Washington (nbcwashington.com)

[63] DC department named in Trayon White federal case missing records on violence interrupters (wjla.com)

the program. Wasted tax dollars. And just like D.C. crime is unchecked, the streets are laden with homeless. Ridden with the smell of urine and feces. For taxpayers, a zero-sum gain.

The borders have allowed the flood of illegal aliens or the new politically correct term… newcomers, into our country with no knowledge of their destinations, or intent. Most welcomed into sanctuary cities. The sanctuary cities opening their arms to MS13 and Venezuelan gangs, their reins of terror stretching law enforcement to their limits. Law enforcement agencies are still unable to recruit officers. Both gangs are extremely violent. The Biden administration ignored public safety in this country. Thankfully the Trump administration has returned public safety to America.

Reality

The only true strategy is to saturate these cities with law enforcement, return SQF as a police tool. Remove the ideological failure of "Catch and Release" or face the consequence that more and more innocent civilians will become the victims of unchecked violence by illegals. The strategy and way ahead are not a difficult decision unless you have blinders on. What is significant is that SQF was not an indiscriminate practice. It was results driven and achieved the intended purpose. The strategy was a success. Officers enforced their sworn duties to protect the people. It was politicians meddling in policing that changed fair and equitable policing that placed the wedge between the police and minority communities.

The sad truth is that evidence collected through the National Crime Victimization Survey (NCVS) specific to the use of weapons in the commission of a crime clearly points to one demographic. The results are consistent with the trends of violent crime across the nation during the past five decades. Black males were more likely to use guns for self-defense in the commission of a crime in urban areas. Most associated with an assault or robberies. The same demographic are also the <u>victims</u> of gun violence. Sixty-one percent black youths (ages fifteen to twenty-four). A societal dilemma.

Politics and the desire to remain in power seem to have overridden the sacred oaths of office. Regardless of political gamesmanship one thing is crystal clear… police strategies need to be bold. Complacency or political wobbling does nothing to affect law and order. Urban cities who support *defund the police* are either intoxicated, or live in a proverbial bubble, far removed from reality. The blood of victims of crime is on their hands. and it can't be washed off. There is only one solution, return law enforcement to the police, allow them to enforce the law.

Chapter 17 – Training

Officers elaborated on broken windows that was presented in the police academy. New York State (NYS) penal law 140.50 (DCJS, 1996) allows officers to temporarily question a person whom the officer has found in public and believed might be armed with a weapon. Officers were well versed in broken windows theory as being synonymous with the methodology behind SQF.

Officers stated that field training upon graduation from the academy is less than adequate. Officers felt that they did not have sufficient time to integrate with the community, gain cultural awareness, and learn *how the game was played*. Officers stated that the assignment of a field training officer (FTO) might be as long as six weeks or as little as five days. Several officers stated that because of their precinct workload that they were released on patrol within several days. The recommended time for an officer to be assigned a FTO, per the NYS Department of Criminal Justice Services is… six months. Officers also stated that no FTO evaluations were performed to assess their field performance.

The academy provides the academic foundation to be a basically trained police officer. You are given police theory, tactics, and procedures in a classroom. The academy engrains the tenets of courtesy, professionalism, and respect. The academics of policing. The FTO provides the practical experience, the second phase… the classroom… the street. FTO training is the graduate course. The practical phase. Officers trained how to deal with "the street," and to make split second life or death decisions. Without proper FTO training, new officers are placed at a disadvantage, vulnerable to poor decisions that may cause irreparable harm to the officer, the community and department.

Many officers were disheartened, stating that their FTO's believed that the community was the enemy. Them Against Us. Another shortcoming is increasing workloads created by the increase in crime. FTO's should be screened, interviewed, and selected by the Precinct Commander. Avoiding that trap is the downfall of community policing. An attitude that an unvetted FTO can easily provide the mentorship to integrate into the community and learn the "street smarts" to be effective, fair, contributing to the development of trust and police legitimacy.

The FTO is a professor. They provide an education for the officers to develop their own perceptions and hone their skills. And during the FTO experience, officers are expected to develop their own critical thinking skills and develop their own sense of community engagement. An officer whose FTO taught him *them against us* reflected on how the community became less concerned about being a victim of crime. Their number one concern… fear of the police. One black resident of Brownsville summed it up.

> *"So, safety concerns switched from fear of the criminal to the police stopping me, and the fear of not just me, but the fear of police stopping my son is a big one. So now you have people in the community saying, I fear the police are stopping my son."*

The FTO should be certified by the state and should be *fenced*. Unable to be reassigned unless there is an absolute emergency. Work from the state FTO guidelines, modified with interjection of department requirements. Train to the standard. When you provide ad hoc FTO training and deviate from the FTO curriculum, the recruit, the community and department all bear the brunt of failed police training.

Education also had a direct impact influencing an officer's decision to initiate SQF. Data collected by the NYPD in 2006 from five hundred six thousand stops examined fifteen hundred randomly selected SQF incidents[64]. What was validated… most officer's decision-making process was not based on race. The study integrated relevant data other than race to determine what triggered an officer's behavior in initiating stops. The trend was based on what they learned in the Academy: precinct crime rates, known high crime areas, time of day (more crimes are committed at night), fugitive movements, suspect behavior, proximity to the crime scene. Not one element based on race or ethnicity.

Officer education continues throughout their career, it's ongoing. Every day an officer learns something new… from the street, from another police officer, from their own ongoing skill development. Maintaining officer proficiency and professionalism is a priority of police departments. Training remains the lifeblood of all departments… with one goal… to protect and serve.

---

[64] New York Police Department (NYPD) Stop, Question, and Frisk Database, 2006 (umich.edu)

Chapter 18 – Impact on Crime

The National Crime Victimization Survey shows that between 1990 and 2018 SQF events had a direct impact on reducing crime. The results were consistent with findings from thirty randomized studies also reporting a modest impact on crime reduction. The NYPD achieved its desired intent; reducing violent crime, and based on systemic analysis, until SQF was curtailed in 2014, an effective deterrent. Fast forward to 2024. The advent of BLM and *defund the police*. Communities of color protesting police racism. In 2024 MSN reported on crime in the underrepresented black communities of NYC. What has the impact of *defund the police* in New York City's minority communities? The results of an MSN survey provide a crushing reality[65].

Brownsville Brooklyn

Brownsville Brooklyn has been infamous for years. The crime rate here is four times higher than the city average. According to statistics, the probability that you will become a victim of an assault here is one in thirty-six. Bodies pile up due to domestic violence and drug-related feuds. This area has resisted the gentrification seen in other parts of Brooklyn (gentrification is the change in the character of a district from one inhabited by tenants from various social groups to an area dominated by residents with high status).

New York photographer Reed Young describes this part of the city saying: *if you're over twenty-five in Brownsville, you're either dead, in prison or have decided to quit gangster life. It's better not to fall into any of those categories and avoid Brownsville.*

South Bronx

The South Bronx, including Mott Haven and Hunts Point, has historically been a working-class neighborhood. It's easy to get into trouble here. The causes are long-standing poverty, gangster traditions, and sex working. According to statistics, there are about five thousand acts of violence per one hundred thousand residents—murders, rapes, assaults, thefts. It's no wonder that the Bronx is the cinematic embodiment of a sinful city. However, it's better not to test this popular opinion on your own skin.

Bedford-Stuyvesant Brooklyn

Bedford-Stuyvesant Brooklyn has been topping the rankings of dangerous NYC neighborhoods for years. Here, it's easy to fall victim to a robbery or get involved in aggressive discussions with locals that can end badly.

Midtown Manhattan

Yes, it's not a mistake - you also need to be cautious in the center of Manhattan. While avoiding this part of NYC is complicated and unfortunate, one can't overlook its dangers. NYC has been struggling with a homelessness crisis for years. People deprived of means of survival in desperation can resort to theft or violence. You should watch out for pickpockets, avoid

---

[65] https://www.msn.com/

deserted alleyways, or empty subway tunnels late at night. When something throws the city off balance, like a power outage, it's better not to leave your home or hotel.

East Harlem

Located within Manhattan, Harlem has a colorful culture and churches where you can listen to gospel choirs. However, going there in a group and during the day is better. The relatively safe area is 125th Street and adjacent ones, thanks to gentrification and tourist popularity. In other parts, the chances of encountering trouble from residents are one in twenty-two. Experienced travelers suggest zipping bags and backpacks, not flaunting expensive gear or jewelry, and not stopping to take photos. It's best to blend into the crowd and open your eyes. These rules will work throughout NYC.

In New York, violence happens in broad daylight, and no one reacts, says one of the dwellers. *From the windows, I saw groups of people looting clothing stores. They just smashed the windows, went in, and took the goods. It went on and on. No one did anything; the police didn't come for hours.* Smash and grab… out of control, especially in our nation's capital. Washington, D.C. a smash and grab is just another night on the town. The police, unaware of the crime happening right in front of their eyes.[66] Lawlessness the new norm. Our nation in a quandary of political deceit.

I will make a bold assumption that twenty years from now, the lawlessness will not have changed. With pandering politicians manipulating the poor and destitute in the same underrepresented communities for personal and political gain.

---

[66] five in custody after burglary spree across multiple City Center DC, Georgetown area businesses (wjla.com)

Chapter 19 – The Way Ahead

Was SQF effective… should it be reintroduced as a tool to control gun violence? That is the question. You be the judge. But the facts are clear… our nation is on a course to exceed the numbers of homicides in NYC in 1990… twenty-six hundred. Broken Windows and Zero Tolerance turned the tide of violent crime in New York. By 2003 NYC, once one of the most dangerous cities in America in the early 1990s, in less than a decade … called the "Safest City in the World."

Since the events of 2020, the country has reversed course. Violent crime is politically acceptable, under the new wave that swept the country… defund the police. With open border policies, a wave of illegal immigrants is creating more policing problems. Now, zero tolerance refers to the inability of the police to arrest and district attorneys to prosecute. Citizens are unprotected. A new generation of social media warriors supporting criminal reform. Looking to eliminate incarceration.

And yes, facts are indisputable, the current incarcerated population is ninety-four percent African American. The political explanation, that all police are systematically racist. The reality, the police are not the gestapo. Arrested and incarcerated because they have been found guilty of committing a crime. Factually it is disproportionate to the rest of the racial demographics of the country. Politicians in a fog, drinking an ideological Kool-Aid. The solution, unity of effort to change the statistics. No consequence in putting criminals back on the streets to commit more crime. Politicians believing ideologies will somehow be welcomed by American citizens. Where is the common sense? Hopefully as the nation has spoken, and elected a pro-law enforcement President, the nation will begin to heal

Demanding that everyone accept policing through the lens of Diversity Equity and Inclusion (DEI). Everyone, fall in line. In less than three years DEI has self-imploded. The same ideology was peddled in the 1960s under the banner of Affirmative Action. The same communist theology spread across the nation then and now. In the 60s it was communes, everyone equal, drugs, living together in harmony. No crime, no concept of how to sustain basic human needs. The counter-revolution. The Make, Love Not War generation.

In the end, the 1960s social revolution sparked by the Viet Nam War failed. The hype and ideology unsustainable. The reality, the communist experiment, the American manifesto failed. Reality and common sense returning to the American psyche. Today this haze of communist ideology is hovering over this country, under the DEI mantra. Politicians believing that crime adheres to ideologies, rhetoric or party politics. Not true. It may be racially disproportionate. Let's be honest, crimes are committed by individuals. It's the individual that make the decision to cross over the threshold from law abiding citizen to criminal. And let's dispel the systematic racism theory. Cops are color blind. They enforce the law and arrest those who intentionally and willfully violate the law.

Since 2020 American citizens of all walks of life, all races and ethnicities are, now *second-class citizen*s. A segment of left-wing politicians blatantly ignoring the *needs of the people*. Long since forgetting that they were elected as the servants of the people. Americans feeling insecure and unsafe. Their ideology, shear insanity, has destroyed our urban cities and continues to drift into our suburbs. A cancer that has metastasized. To save this nation it must be stopped.

Antisemitism and anti-American hatred openly spewed on our streets and in our "prestigious" universities. Acts of terrorism. It's effected the efficiency of our industries, and instilled wokeness in our military. The constitution and the rule of law were viciously attacked.

What is the national priority… criminal and social justice reform, or the protection, safety, and security of citizens. Crime in urban communities has gone from bad to worse. No more than active War Zones. Chicago and St. Louis. the most dangerous cities in the nation. Washington, D.C, our nation's capital, decimated by violent crime, for the second year (2023 - 2024) listed as the most undesirable city to live in the United States[67]. NYC… a pandemic of migrant crime and homelessness. The national crime rate as of September 2024 up thirty-seven percent.[68]

Washington, D.C., the first urban community to jump on the Black Lives Matter racial equity bandwagon in 2020. Muriel Bowser memorializing downtown D.C., designating Black Lives Matter Plaza.[69] A street painted in huge yellow letters demonstrating black pride. While just a few blocks away in the communities of Southeast and Northwest, crime rampant… school shootings, carjackings, violent attacks on innocent people, smash and grabs. Violent crime, just another day in the "District." Innocent black residents, especially children, victims of this scourge. What changed in D.C. and other urban communities? Crime is allowed to occur with the police understaffed, their hands tied, by laws favoring criminals. Aggressive policing, stop question and frisk forbidden and dismissed as systemic racism.

The police across urban enterprises are unable to curb incessant violent crime. Parents whose children have been victims of senseless gun violence grieving for the loss of a child. Living in shooting galleries. BLM signs should be removed. What should be honored are the names of those innocents killed by urban thugs. In our nation's capital the BLM mural should be replaced by the words "Black Lives Killed in the District," the letters BLKIDC painted in "*Blood Red*." With a ten-foot-high digital meter, clicking away as the numbers of innocent D.C. residents are needlessly killed. Like the continued federal deficit in the trillions, the numbers will continue rise and rise and rise, never ending.

In D.C., rhetoric to appease the community. The Mayor and Chief of Police holding endless community meetings. Taking crime walks (surrounded by protective details) … then quickly exiting the danger zone. Leaving residents to fend for themselves… returning to their posh offices and homes far from the violence. Like Sharpton, and Holder did in Ferguson, get the photo op, apologize to black community for overzealous racist police, spew racist rhetoric, then walk away.

---

[67] https://www.msn.com/en-us/news/us/new-study-ranks-this-us-city-as-the-least-desirable-to-live-in-for-a-second-year-running/a
[68] Latest DOJ data shows crime rates remain elevated under Biden - Washington Times
[69] https://www.washington.org-visitd.c.-black lives matter plaza

But I believe that there is light at the end of the tunnel. The public tired of crime, and even more disconcerting… the results of the 2024 elections. The American people have spoken. Kansas City Mayor Quinton Lucas, who previously supported *defunding the police* efforts, is now pushing to increase patrols in areas reeling from ongoing criminal behavior after the deadly shooting of a popular chef left the community reeling.[70] Another hypocrisy as Lucas, in May 2024, the state of Missouri denied application for Kansas City to become a sanctuary city. Yet Lucas unofficially bypassed their decision. Openly inviting illegals to flood the city plagued with crime. The community concerned, with the standard response by the city administration.[71]

In New York, Adams is so desperate he's brought back a new version of the Street Crimes Unit (SCU). Neighborhood Safety Teams (NSTs).[72] New name for the same mission. Get guns off the street. The difference is that NSTs are not undercover, they are in uniform. And where are they being deployed… to the same high crime precincts that the SCU worked. With the same result… challenged and charged with overaggressive searches, targeting minorities. The NSTs of this generation, facing the same scrutiny, accused of making unconstitutional stops.

The Monitor's September 4, 2024, Edition[73], reported *Terry* stops increased slightly from ten percent of stops in 2021 to eleven percent of stops in 2022. Unconstitutional frisks rose from fifteen percent of all frisks in 2021 to twenty-four percent of all frisks in 2022, an over fifty percent increase. Unlawful searches also rose significantly, by almost fifty percent, from twenty percent of all searches in 2021 to thirty percent of all searches in 2022. In the first half of 2023, twelve percent of reported *Terry* stops were unconstitutional, thirty-one percent of frisks were unconstitutional, and thirty-three percent of searches were unconstitutional.

Déjà vu, as reported in the 1990s by the NYCLU during the SQF era, that the SCU's were making more improper *Terry* stops than patrol units. This trend has continued. For example, the Monitor team found that *Terry* stops related to 9-1-1 calls conducted by patrol officers in the first half of 2023 were lawful in ninety-one percent of reports reviewed. In the same period, the specialized units, such as the Neighborhood Safety Teams (NSTs) and Public Safety Teams (PSTs), made fifty-four percent of improper *Terry* stops.

---

[70] https://www.foxnews.com/us/blue-city-mayor-who-supported-defund-police-movement-calls-more-officers-after-popular-chefs-murder

[71] Rising crime in KC discussed at BOPC meeting Tuesday (fox4kc.com)

[72] NYPD Neighborhood Safety Teams Engaged in Illegal Stops (nymag.com)

[73] New York Police Department Monitor, *Nineteenth Report of the Independent Monitor*, NYPD MONITOR (June 5, 2023), available at https://www.nypdmonitor.org/wp-content/uploads/2023/06/NST-Report.pdf.

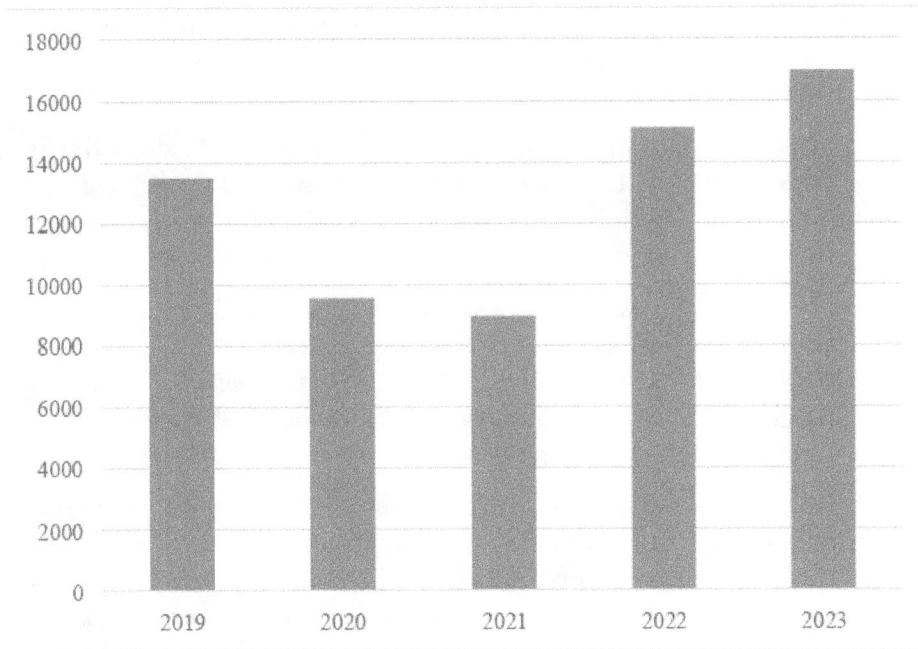

Table 6 - Relative *Terry* Stops, 2019 - 2023

The return of pro-active policing. Politically correct… no. At the very least, regardless of political design, taking action to reduce crime and keep communities safe.

If the country is to survive and our citizens provided *Life, Liberty and the Pursuit of Happiness*, guaranteed by the Declaration of Independence, dramatic reversals in police policy need to happen… NOW. Equally apply the law to citizens, native born, naturalized, even illegal aliens whose immigration status has yet to be determined by the courts. With the caveat that they obey the law. They are guaranteed these protections. Bring back common-sense policing. The current political solution… kick the can down the road. Gun control bills are no more than useless pieces of paper that have ZERO influence on reducing gun violence on the street.

New York State Law 140.50 - Temporary Questioning of Persons in Public Places; Search for Weapons is a standing law. It wasn't created for the purpose of targeting communities of color. It was one of the multiple enforcement tools available to the police to take guns off the streets. Was it successful… absolutely. Shootings plummeted from fourteen thousand in 1993 to a record low of thirty-five hundred in 2009. Those numbers remained steady for more than a decade, directly attributed to the broken windows theory, SQF and Zero tolerance. Those same urban communities now suffer equally abhorrent crime. This is the effect from elitist ideological political stupidity.

Defunding the police was nothing more than politicians placing the police on *lockdown*. This started the domino effect. Now the officer, not the department, is open to lawsuits by a suspect, for claims of misconduct. Police caught between the rock and a hard place, in a dire situation. Be aggressive and risk being sued. Ferguson effect policing. Be reactive… respond and report.

Illegal immigration further challenges officers. Hampered by no cash bail, now having to fight a war against criminals, both foreign and domestic. Underrepresented communities are still the scapegoats of political manipulation.

The effect of *defunding the police*. During the SQF era officers knew the department had their backs. Today they know they don't have their back. They know that they'd be thrown under the bus - held liable in civil proceedings. One officer summed up his frustration and of thousands of officers across the nation:

> *"I believe if you do something with good intention, and you're not malicious about it, this job should back you up. It does not. Their question is "why did you stop him? What was your reason for stopping him? Okay, but that's fine, you stopped him for this reason, then why did you search him? Did you put your hands in his pocket and pull out the gun?" They'll question everything you do, but they push you to do it. I don't want to get sued, so why should I put my neck out for this job if the job's not going to back me up."*

Since *defund the police* criminals have declared open season on the police. And the police sit idly by stymied by meaningless policies. On patrol with targets on their backs. In 2023 there were one hundred thirty-six police officers killed in the line of duty. A decrease of thirty-nine percent, yet that same year three hundred seventy-eight were shot by perpetrators, an increase of fourteen percent. [74] The police are in self-preservation mode. Unfortunately, statistics paint the same decades old picture… index crimes, especially gun violence remain exclusively in communities of color. Black on black shooting, but a new ruthless category… illegal migrants is growing. Tren de Aragua openly taking over communities in Aurora, Colorado. And the political rhetoric… there is no issue. Sanctuary city Mayors using their magical crystal balls providing political *cover their ass* statistics. Denying there is a problem. Violating the constitution by harboring illegal immigrants.

Today gangs control the street, and truancy is out of control. Thirty-six percent of NYC students chronically miss more than ten percent of school. In D.C., an even worse case, a deplorable sixty percent chronic truancy. Where are the parents? Two lost generations. Guns readily available through the criminal network, especially online "ghost guns." Untraceable, no serial numbers. Obtained through the mail. Guns are the method of conflict resolution in black communities. The street solution, no more than false bravado. *Defund the police* assuring that criminals are emboldened, no longer afraid of the police or consequences. Insanity. Unfortunately for many... the rite of passage to establish self-worth in the concrete jungle.

Respect for life, values and ethics taught in the home and church … long since evaporated. In these communities the issue is no longer racial targeting and illegal search. Surviving random shootings and living in fear are their daily life and death challenges. The cry for the return of the police is muffled by the same pandering politicians promising change. Aggressive policing is what the citizenry wants. Yes… the return of broken windows policing.

When will public administrators change their policies for the best interest of the community and provide policies that have public value? Will they ever consider the needs, safety, security and attitudes of the community when investing public funds in programs and policy? Or will

---

[74] Fewer police officers died in the line of duty in 2023, but 'scary number' were shot: Study (usatoday.com)

they continue to push policies that they know are unenforceable? Destined to fail, band-aid fixes. False promises while death looms in these underrepresented communities… every day.

Urban cities need to generate successful programs to reverse the conditions that have plagued the downward spiral of atrocious socio-economic conditions. Urban communities where little or no success has been achieved to stem the tide of poverty and crime for decades. Let's make that point clear… changing the face of the community is not a police role. But police do have an impact and are a contributor on how to initiate effective community police strategies. The police and sociologists continue to identify the direct correlation between socio-economic conditions and crime. Yet, regardless of multiple studies and recommended courses of action, they are ignored by politicians. Why… they don't help get votes.

Schools have failed the urban community. The ability to master the basic skills are well below the national average. Public schools prepare them for a one-way path to the street… selling drugs, committing violent crimes and incarceration. The media captures the plight of the community… demanding action. Politicians respond with useless rhetoric. Politicians' agendas… to identify *the root cause*. The root cause of the socio-economic blight that leads to crime. Kicked down the road for decades. Used by politicians to keep underrepresented constituents on the hook of dependence.

Our borders remain porous. The continued influx of foreign criminals, human trafficking and fentanyl continue to decimate the path of least resistance… the minority communities. We're headed in the direction of self-destruction. The country is at a point where the *defund the police* experiment has failed, and we need to reverse course and reinstate law and order, or… face the end of America as a free democracy. Hopefully that transition will be in the process very soon as we move from a destroy to a make America great again administration.

If not organized law enforcement will be replaced by citizen militias protecting their homes and communities from the invasion of crime. And the root cause as in all failed democracies, the elites, the phonies, the politicians, all interested in power and personal gain. Florida has taken a stance on crime and is unapologetic. Florida sheriffs have openly directed members of the community to arm themselves. They are supporting citizens to use deadly physical force to protect themselves and their property from criminals. Criminals are put on notice. Why? Because the *defund the police* movement has affected staffing levels and response times. Citizens under the second amendment have the right to defend themselves. In essence, unity of effort that achieves community policing.

Nassau County, New York looking to deputize gun owners as part of an emergency response force.[75] Progressive politicians, who play a shell game to bamboozle the public, performing the standard political tap dance… show up for the photo op, act as if they care, make speeches, shake a few hands and walk away. Let's review the most relevant example.

In Ferguson, Missouri, after the Michael Brown shooting, Reverand Al Sharpton and President Obama's attorney general, Eric Holder came to Ferguson. Holder apologizing to the community for the aggressive "racist police." Sharpton going on about the plight of African

---

[75] New York county executive plans to 'deputize' select gun owners (msn.com)

American's and years of oppression from racist cops. They made their political statements, got their photo op and disappeared. Further igniting racial tensions, intentionally. Making useless promises how the government was going to improve the socio-economic condition of this destitute crime infested community. All while stores and property were looted and destroyed by the Ferguson community. The Department of Justice mandating the police department diversify to better represent the community and applying soft on crime (look the other way) practices. Ferguson remains a socio-economic disaster, still reeling from poverty and crime. Nothing has changed, and politicians are nowhere to be found.

The 2020 social revolution after the killing of George Floyd spawned the *defund the police* movement. Politicians mustered on the steps of the capital building, took to social media, and showed their support… "taking a knee." Jumping on the Black Lives Matter (BLM) movement. BLM raked in millions. What went to the black communities… nothing. The money was funneled into their own pockets. BLM's promises to help black underrepresented communities was nothing but a lie. Minority communities are the scapegoat of this scam. The BLM manifesto,[76] lies, fraud and embezzlement. Politicians riding the bandwagon, blindly beating the drum of anti-police rhetoric. And when it all went bad, crawling back into the capital building. Action taken… zero. Political hypocrisy.

What has happened to these communities? Have any positive changes been made? No. Two things have changed… for the worse. One… surges in violent crime… and continued economic decline. With all the left-wing saber rattling… where is Ferguson today? In 2024 the violent crime rate in Ferguson is one hundred seventeen percent above the national average. One hundred forty-six violent crimes committed in Ferguson during 2023. The crime statistics remain appalling.

Ten years since Ferguson became a pillar of racial justice, it remains destitute. The rabble rousers came and went. The same deplorable statistics follow suit in urban underrepresented communities across the nation. The decades old revolving door of crime and destroyed infrastructure.

What has changed is how black mayors have now not only *defunded the police* but defunded social programs for black residents. Redirecting millions to illegal migrants to pad the political voting blocks. Chicago a war zone. The Black community intentionally pushed aside by the saviors of Chicago's black community… Mayors Lightfoot and Johnson. Crucifying black residents. Moving funds from taxpaying constituents, to pay for housing, medical care, and other social programs for migrants. Looking to pursue amnesty to secure political control in perpetuity. The black community pushed further down the food chain. Held hostage, nothing more than political slavery! .

What can be done. When is the safety and security of our communities going to outweigh race and *woke* politics? When will the government care about innocent lives? When are the police going to be allowed to restore law and order? When will the National Guard be mobilized to fight to stop the foreign invasion? One of the Guard's primary state missions is to

---

[76] After Raising $90 Million in 2020, Black Lives Matter Has $42 Million in Assets - The New York Times (nytimes.com)

mitigate civil disturbance. Just as they did during hurricane Katrina in 2005, and the U.S. Capital following the January 6th, 2021, riots. Yet with soft on crime policies, the last thing politicians want to do is admit their communities are under siege. Are politicians held accountable… maybe, when hell freezes over. Negligence at the highest levels.

Elected officials in unison openly violate their oaths of office. They swore *to defend the constitution of their State and constitution of the United States against all enemies foreign and domestic*. For politicians just words. Ignorance is bliss, using the system solely for personal and political gain. Now our foreign and domestic enemies are here. We are occupied by illegals whose intent can only be speculated. An occupation army operating in plain sight. And we're funding their operations. Unlike politicians, our first responders and military hold themselves accountable to their departments, communities and the nation. Maintaining their sacred oaths.

We're off course, political agenda overriding common sense policing. Adding to the dynamic social dysfunction, especially in underserved communities. The nation, states and localities remain divided politically and along racial lines. Unless the nation returns to *common sense policing* and elected leaders and stakeholders (political, community, law enforcement) turn this disaster around, America is doomed. A house divided cannot stand, neither can a house where anarchy and chaos prevail. Without common sense law enforcement practices, crime will lead to vigilantism to the point that democracy will dissolve. We have one opportunity to unite a nation in disarray before states that make up the United States of America will secede to form more perfect unions.

Chapter 20 – A Country on Notice

The country is on the verge of imploding. The great experiment of a nation of the people by the people and for the people… will perish from this earth. States and localities will close ranks and form independent governments. States having no choice but to cut ties with a government of elites for the elites. Their allegiance… not the people they swear to protect and serve, but to their political party and left-wing drive to form a socialist state.

A nation needs law and order to function and maintain national stability. Without that basic thread, there is no nation, only corruption, anarchy and chaos. One thing is clear, the political football of race will always be engrained in our political system. It can't be escaped. Race is a political platform. Law and order and politics have nothing to do with enforcing the law.

This is extremely difficult when politicians representing communities of color use race like a game show. They clamor about the inequities of the Black community at public gatherings… and election time. They ignore their community's plight and forget their constituents in between elections, unless they need to use race to pursue some political issue.

In schools, fascist propaganda, through the lens of critical race theory, clouds the minds of our children, projecting racial hatred, building resentment and anger. Radical ideology eliminating qualifications for racial efficacy and efficiency through quotas is a sound business – government practice. Thank god our country is finally throwing this radical concept where it belongs… in the garbage.

Weapons are being brought into schools. School resource officers are a threat to students… their presence upsetting minority students… until there is a shooting, stabbing or violent riot. Officers are admonished if they use their experience to execute probable suspicion searches and take guns off the street, police racism. Students are assaulting teachers and other students. Punishment… a slap on the wrists or zero consequence. Schools are chaotic. In many schools learning is secondary… survival is the priority. Who's in charge of the zoo?

SQF was controversial… no question. The foundation of attacking crime was founded in the *Broken Windows* theory. This was relevant in the 1990s as it is today. It is an unbiased crime reduction theory validated by the NYPD during the two decades of the SQF Era. Cops… of all races and ethnicities enforced SQF. And as with all societies, there are a segment of those entrusted to enforce the law, who abused their positions of authority. You can't escape that. From the minority officers I interviewed, and the result of the independent Rand Report… that number was exceedingly small. What was relevant is that once officers put on the uniform, they left their personal prejudices and attitudes in their lockers. They did the job of enforcing the law. Cops patrol the streets with targets on their back. And they are targeted not only by pandering politicians, but by revolving door criminals. God bless their commitment to the communities and each other.

NYC's zero tolerance and SQF initiative were never meant to be a social justice experiment. There was one goal and one goal only, the reduction of gun violence. But the measure of success is a state of mind, not just numbers and statistics. Officers defined the measure of success by the communities' overall feeling of peace and safety. Officers unanimously indicated that community involvement is a critical variable in the equation. In the Stop Question and Frisk Era the city felt peace and safety. Reinvigorated NYC returned to a vibrant hub of tourism. The economy boomed. NYC returned to being the center of the universe. SQF and the introduction of common-sense policing… a significant factor of NYC's rebirth.

The cry for diversity has been achieved. Migration to New York has evolved over the past three decades. Most New York City residents are non-Caucasian. As the city changed so did the city civil servants. The NYPD remains approximately fifty-three percent of minority sworn officers. But be careful, don't fall into the false narrative. Diversity does not make a good police department. First and foremost, people join the police department… because they want to be a cop. They want to perform the job. They want to protect and serve… not make a social statement. There is no equity if my partner's focus is on being a spokesperson for racial justice and cannot keep up in a foot chase or handcuff a perp. Lowering standards is not the answer. I certainly don't want that person, male or female, straight or gay to be my partner. Your misguided social justice will get me killed!

What should never be compromised are the standards to be a physically fit, dedicated and loyal officer. In fact, entry requirements should be made more rigid. Why… to be able to meet the mental and physical stress of the job. The payoff for maintaining high standards? A professional law enforcement officer mentally and physically capable of performing the rigors of a very demanding job.

You must recruit the best and brightest, the most dedicated, loyal, motivated people. You're a public figure. Police Officers don't only make arrests. They are part of the community. They wear many hats, psychologist, mentor, enforcer. Being a police officer is not about racial equity. It's a commitment of selfless service to your oath and the community you serve and protect. The police department is a *Band of Brothers and Sisters* in Blue. Accepting anything less places officers and the community in peril.

The NYPD expanded its horizons as did most urban departments. Neighborhood Policing. Policing that unifies relationships between the police and community, engaging in efforts to bridge cultural gaps. Like any policy or program that is attempting to validate its public value, it had and continues to have many flaws and weaknesses. The objective remains the same. Professionalism is critical. Because the community will judge the officers who go into the community. And they will immediately know which officers care and whom they can trust. The best barometer of how a department is doing is not CompStat, or the FBI Uniformed Crime Reports. It's the perception of the community. That's the measure of success or failure. And here's a flash… the community doesn't care the color of an officer. They want to feel safe; they want criminals arrested.

We have gone full circle. Once revered, the police are now vilified. Once actively engaged in preventive policing, through stop question and frisk, officers are now reluctant to engage. Fearing for their own lives and financial ruin. Yet they continue to step up to do their jobs, running towards the danger. They realize they are the glue that holds society together from anarchy and lawlessness.

Stop Question and Frisk is an effective police *tool*. Regardless of the racial controversy and complaints of overzealous enforcement. SQF was a societal wish from the City of New York to regain control of a city ravaged by gun violence, during the crack cocaine epidemic of the 80s. The use of SQF dramatically changed course when politicians played cop and tarnished the shield… mandating SQF quotas. Politicians continue to tarnish the shield. The polarizing division of mistrust between the community and police created *a them against us* psyche.

CompStat, politicians, bureaucratic manipulation were not what took guns off the street. NYC went from despair to the *Greatest City in the Universe*. It was the street cop enforcing the law, using SQF to aggressively get guns off the street. Making split second decisions to keep citizens safe. Using officer discretion, and probable suspicion. Dealing with the homeless, vagrants, druggies, emotionally disturbed persons (EDPs), and violent offenders. Just as they do today. It was the minority patrol officer that was caught between the rock and a hard place, as they are now. Faced with the dilemma of empathy for the underrepresented communities they patrol and their loyalty to the departments they serve. A heavy emotional burden to shoulder.

One officer captured SQF in a nutshell. His comment was resounding back in 2000 as it should be today.

> *"Most people want to live in a safe place, a safe environment. So how do we address it, how do we make this place safe? That was a tool that came about, so it's not like it was made with malicious intent; it was made to address an issue and addressing that issue was demanded by all sides."*

Elected officials and public administrators must be held accountable for developing sound public policies relevant to public need. And if they violate that sacred trust, held accountable. The concept is simple. And when policies are made, do not leave out ground level people who get the job done. They are the foundation of any policy.

Officers were extremely frustrated, excluded from being part of the policy process. Historically in departments across the nation, policy decisions have been reserved for those at the senior police level, politicians, and political appointees. Not having ever experienced what officers deal with on the street. No clue of how programs affect policing. Relying solely on statistical data. Bureaucrats with zero understanding of the effectiveness and public value of a taxpayer funded program. Bureaucrats do not examine all the community and public variables. How will a policy affect the demographics and culture of the community? What is the intended public value? You can't attain that information sitting in plush office. That comes from the officers who live and interface with the community and have firsthand knowledge of the "variables." A shot in the arm of common sense. And with SQF, what was the profit margin for improved public safety by removing SQF and other pro-active police strategies? Have departments' stock market value jumped or are they on the brink or becoming bankrupted by poor investment strategy.

Law enforcement will never be accepted with open arms. Especially by those who are violating the law. One group or another will raise the mantle of discrimination. It happens across the globe. Every race and ethnicity have issues with how they are treated by the police. No one in the community accepts blame for criminal activity. The blame for all crime, as always, rests on the shoulders of overzealous or under zealous police. That aspect of transference has been around since the beginning of time.

The question is simple… will each of the stakeholders do their jobs? Will politicians write fair and common-sense policies for the community? Will underrepresented communities become solvent and culturally prosperous? Politicians' jobs, not the police. Will they bear the mantel of responsibility and accountability for the socio-economic distress of forgotten communities? Will the police be allowed to take vicious criminals off the street? Will ludicrous policies such as no cash bail be stricken? Will the community assume the roles of mentors? Will parents supervise and parent their children, protecting them from the dangers of crime. Helping them to have a chance for a future. And will the triad stakeholders, the elders; the police, the community, elected officials, come to the table with an earnest desire to create police policies in the best interest of the community, the states, and the nation? Will they be held accountable?

Chapter 21 – Conclusion - Liberation

The pendulum has begun to swing. When I started to write this book, in 2024, the nation was in a quagmire of lawlessness. The borders were open, and a deluge of illegals, terrorists, and criminal gangs were flooding our nation. Unvetted, free to commit crimes against US citizens. Policies intended to pad the US Census and change the constitution to give illegals the right to vote. Cementing one-party rule for perpetuity. Elitists free to rein, constituent voices silenced.

Today we are in the process of rebuilding our nation. Liberated from the Biden debacle. This book was written to provide a comparative analysis of the effectiveness of Stop Question and Frisk in the 1990's Guliani Era. Providing the relevance to common sense policing, returning the tools of law enforcement to our local, state and federal law enforcement agencies. Aggressive policing to protect the American Public.

In a John Wayne movie, there is an iconic commentary from Col. Thursday, the commanding officer of the "regiment". Preparing to rejoin his decimated command, he turns to Captain York (John Wayne) professing…. "When you command this regiment…and you probably will… COMMAND IT". As the commander in chief, Donald Trump is doing just this. Leading from the front, identifying threats against this nation…and Commanding. We have not had a President with such a weight of the collapse of this nation on their shoulders since Abraham Lincoln.

He saw through the smoke and mirrors of the lies projected by manipulated crime statistics in D.C. He assessed the situation and made a "command decision". He federalized the D.C. National Guard and federal law enforcement to rid the nation's capital of crime. Regardless of the protests from D.C.'s failed leadership and opposing explosive rhetoric from the opposition. He identified the criminal threat to the American people…and took action. The result…more than 400 arrests, in just the first few days of the operation. The people of D.C. come out of their homes, from self-imposed isolation. Thanking law enforcement.

Like President Lincoln, who ended slavery by issuing the Emancipation Proclamation, President Trump should also be praised as an Emancipator. Who has been impacted by the rampant crime? The black and underrepresented community. Not only in D.C. but in every democratic city across the nation. His dramatic executive actions have reinforced the rule of law.

He has declared "real" war on crime. Tossing the "status quo". Action not words. Protecting American citizens, regardless of race, ethnicity and gender. Enforcing "Federal Law", Still an uphill battle, as it will take time to reverse the damage from the demoralization from sanctuary cities efforts to defund the police, welcoming unvetted criminals, the scum of the earth. Now on notice. The new Sheriff, President Donald Trump, directing what should be coined an "American Transition". We are returning from the depths of the second "American Depression". August 13th, 2025, the Pearl Harbor …and 911 for criminals and the domestic enemies of this country. The President whose mantra should be "Who Let the Dogs Out". And his dogs will not hesitate to bite!!

100

I point out in that during the SQF Era, CompStat provided the metrics of success. The numbers in New York during the Guiliani Administration captured the numbers of index crimes. The "Books" were not cooked. That changed. From my interviews with officers and research once politicians meddled with the statistics, infusing a quota system. CompStat became tarnished. Today, sanctuary cities are reporting record lows in violent crime. D.C. reporting a 30% reduction in violent crime. Which was misleading. It was discovered in D.C. that numbers were manipulated to intentionally show a reduction violent crime. A Captain in the DC Metropolitan Police Department directed to "cook the books".

I guarantee that creative manipulation is an art that is going on in sanctuary cities. Utilizing a playbook of under reporting crime, reducing charges from felonies to misdemeanors. Officers refusing to respond to calls for service, in fear of being civilly prosecuted, or face departmental discipline. Hopefully this new day will return common sense policing. Every sanctuary city warranting a Department of Justice Investigation to determine the statistical reporting procedures, and if their books are also being "flame broiled".

The only administration to incur a Federal Government takeover of local law enforcement was President Lincoln. President Abraham Lincoln invoked martial law during the Civil War, notably suspending the writ of habeas corpus to maintain order and suppress insurrection in various states, including Maryland and Kentucky. This action was controversial and raised significant constitutional questions regarding the limits of presidential power. Allowing the military to enforce domestic law. President Trump has directed the use of the National Guard under his constitutional authority to "Support and Defend the Constitution of the United States Against All Enemies Foreign and Domestic.

And this is not a violation of Posse Comitatus. The US military has deployed under the Defense Support to Civil Authority Act (DSCA), granting the authority for the Secretary of Defense to provide military forces and equipment to "support" law enforcement. An offshoot from the 1950 Federal Civil Defense Act. Using Stop Question and Frisk as just one enforcement tool to remove criminals from the streets of D.C.

I penned this book because of my frustration as a retired police officer. I believe I captured that my frustration and that of the American people are tired and fed up with the dysfunctional law enforcement system. I had no "crystal ball". I was unaware that President Trump and his Cabinet had been planning the "Return of Law Enforcement to the American People". It was mere coincidence that this book mirrored the actions that President Trump has directed to restore transparency to the streets of D.C.

I believe that President Trump is heard the voices of the American people. "We the People", the American people. Immigrant or native born, we deserve to be safe from crime through ideological enforcement. This is a war being waged across the country. Politically and criminally, it is a war between the forces of good and evil.

The liberation date; August 13, 2025. Yes, a date that will live in infamy. The day our nation started the return of law enforcement to the American people. The Commander in Chief will "Command". And he will use the tools available, to include the proven success of stop question and frisk to remove criminals from the streets and restore order.

Like Mayor Guiliani on steroids, President Trump has done what other Presidents have failed to do. He invoked federal law. Leading from the front to protect the American public. In the process, aggressively placing criminals on notice... all criminals; domestic and foreign.

D.C. may be just the first city using federal statutes to employ the full resources of the government to remove our domestic enemies. We'll see. What we do know is that the left will do everything in their power to treasonously undermine the administration. With abject hatred of the President and the American people.

President Trump is an action-oriented leader. He is a leader, Commands, and has restored "HOPE" to the United States of America.

GOD BLESS THE UNITED STATES OF AMERICA

References

American Civil Liberties Union (2010), *In New York, Be Black (or Latino), Be Stopped, Be Frisked.* Retrieved from https://www.aclu.org/blog/new york be black or latino be stopped be frisked

Avdija, A.S. (2013). Police stop, and frisk practices: An examination of factors that affect officers' decisions to initiate a stop and frisk police procedure. *International Journal of Public Science and Management, 16*(1), 26-35. doi:10.1350/ijps.2014.16.1.325

Baciu, O.A., & Parpucea, I. (2011). Socio-economic factors impact on crime rate. *Review of Economic Studies and Research Virgil Madgearu,* 4(2), 5-20. Retrieved from ProQuest (No. 912511026).

Baumer, E.P., & Wolff, K.T. (2014). Evaluating contemporary crime drops in America, New York City, and many other places. *Justice Quarterly,* 31(1), 5-38. doi:10.1080/07418825.2012.742127

Barbour, R.S., 2000. The role of qualitative research in broadening the "evidence base" for clinical practice. *Journal of Evaluation in Clinical Practice,* 6(2), pp.155–163.

Beckenkamp, M., Engel, C., Glöckner, A., Irlenbusch, B., Hennig-Schmidt, H., Kube, S., Kurschilgen, M., Morell, A., Nicklisch, A., Normann, H., & Towfigh, E. (2009). First impressions are more important than early intervention: Qualifying broken windows theory in the lab. *Max Planck Institute for Research on Collective Goods.* Retrieved from https://www.iame.uni-bonn.de/people/sebastian-kube/workingpapers/2009_21online.pdf

Bell, G.C., Hopson, M.C., Craig, R., & Robinson, N.W. (2014). Exploring black and white accounts of 21st century racial profiling: Riding and driving while black. *Qualitative Research Reports in Communication,* 15, (1), 33-42. doi:10.1080/17459435.2014.955590

Bellin, J. (2014). The inverse relationship between the constitutionality and effectiveness of New York City "stop and frisk." *Boston University Law Review,* 94, 1495-1552. Retrieved from http://scholarship.law.wm.edu/cgi/viewcontent.cgi?article=2745&context=facpub

Boddy, C.R. (2016). Sample size for qualitative research. *Qualitative Market Research: An International Journal,* 19(4), 426-432. doi:10.1108/QMR-06-2016-0053

Boeije, H. (2009). *Analysis in qualitative research.* Thousand Oaks, CA: Sage publications.

Bowen, G.A. (2008). Naturalistic inquiry and the saturation concept: A research note. *Qualitative Research,* 8(1), 137-152. doi:10.1177/1468794107085301

Braga, A.A., & Weisburd, D.L. (2015). Focused deterrence and the prevention of violent gun injuries: Practice, theoretical principles, and scientific evidence. *Annual Review of Public Health,* 36, 55-68. doi:10.1146/annurev-publhealth-031914=122444

Braga, A.A., Welsh, B.C., & Schnell, C. (2015). Can policing disorder reduce crime? A systematic review and meta-analysis. *Journal of Research in Crime and Delinquency,* 52(4), 567-588. doi:10.1177/0022427815576576

Bratton, W.J. & Kelling, G.L. (2015). Why we need broken windows policing. *City Journal*. Retrieved from https://www.city-journal.org/html/why-we-need-broken-windows- policing-13696.html

Bridenball, B., & Jesilow, P. (2008). What matters: The formation of attitudes toward the police. *Police Quarterly*, 11(2), 151-181. doi:10.1177/1098611107313942

Burruss, G.W., & Giblin, M.J. (2014). Modeling Isomorphism on Policing Innovation: The Role of Institutional Pressures in Adopting Community-Oriented Policing. *Crime & Delinquency*, 60(3), 331–355. https://doi.org/10.1177/0011128709340225

Butts, J.A., Roman, C.G., Bostwick, L., & Porter, J.R. (2015). Cure violence: A public health model to reduce gun violence. *Annual Review of Public Health*, 36, 1-20. doi:10.1146/annurev-publhealth-031914-122509

Caelli, K., Ray, L., & Mill, J. (2003). Clear as mud: Toward greater clarity in generic qualitative research. *International Journal of Qualitative Methods*, 2(2), 1-27. doi:10.1177/160940690300200201

Center for Constitutional Rights. (2012). Stop and frisk: The human impact. The stories behind the numbers, the effects on our communities. Retrieved from https://ccrjustice. org/sites/default/files/attach/2015/08/the-human-impact-report.pdf Chambers, S. (2003). Deliberative democratic theory. *Annual Review of Political Science* 6: 307-326

Chambers, S. (2003). Deliberative democratic theory. *Annual Review of Political Science* 6: 307-326

Chaney, C., & Robertson, R.V. (2013). Racism and police brutality in America. *Journal of African American Studies*, 17(4), 478-505. doi:10.1007/s12111-013-9246-5

Charmaz, K. (1996). The search for meanings: Grounded theory. In J.A. Smith, R. Harrè, & L. van Langehove (Eds.). *Rethinking methods in psychology* (pp. 27-49). London: Sage Publications

Chowdhury, M.F. (2015). Coding, sorting, and sifting of qualitative data analysis: Debates and discussion. *Quality & Quantity*, 49(3), 1135-1143. doi:10.1007/s11135-014-0039-2

Clark, G. (2007, April 2). "Black-on-black" policing: Ethnic identification among African Americans. Retrieved from http://sociology.berkeley.edu/sites/default/files/documents/student_papers/Gardner_Clark_BNBPolicing.pdf

CompStat. (2012). Retrieved from https://compstat.nypdonline.org/

CompStat. (2017). Retrieved from https://compstat.nypdonline.org/

CompStat. (2018). Retrieved from https://compstat.nypdonline.org/

Cook, L. (2018, Apr 17). NYPD response to saheed vassell shows need for mental illness overhaul, more community policing, experts say. *AM New York*. Retrieved from https://www.amny.com/news/saheed-vassell-nypd-response-1.18099664

Cordner, G.W. (2014). Community policing elements and effects. In M. Reisig & R. J. Kane (Eds.), *The Oxford handbook of police and policing*, (pp. 432-449). Oxford, UK: Oxford University Press.

Creswell, J.W. (2013). *Qualitative inquiry and research design: Choosing among five approaches* (3rd ed.). Thousand Oaks, CA: Sage.

Culhane, S.E., Bowman, J.H., & Schweitzer, K. (2016). Public perceptions of the justifiability of police shootings: The role of body cameras in a pre- and post- Ferguson experiment. *Police Quarterly*, 19(3), 251-274. doi:10.1177/1098611116651403

Department of Criminal Justice Services (1996). New York state criminal procedures law, article 140, and section 140.50. *Temporary Questioning of persons in public places; searches for weapons*, Albany, NY: New York State office of Criminal Justice Services.

del Carmen, R.V. (2010). *Criminal procedure: Law and practice.* Belmont, CA: Wadsworth, Cengage Learning

Dempsey, J.S. & Forst, L.S. (2010). *Police.* Boston, MA: Cengage Learning.

Dempsey, J.S. & Forst, L.S. (2013). *An introduction to policing* (7th ed.). Boston, MA: Cengage Learning.

Deuchar, R., Fallik, S.W., & Crichlow, V. J. (2018). Despondent officer narratives and the 'post-Ferguson' effect: Exploring law enforcement perspectives and strategies in a southern American state. *Policing and Society: An International Journal of Research and Policy*, 1-16. doi:10.1080/10439463.2018.1480020

Devers, K. & Frankel, R.M. (2000). Study design in qualitative research-2: Sampling and data collection strategies. *Education for Health*, 13(2), 263-271. Retrieved from https://pdfs.semanticscholar.org/0f2a/172dd6c1f790d981abea309e91151815fdb2.pdf

Durose, M.R., Schmitt, E.L., & Langan, P.A. (2005). *Contacts between police and the public: Findings from the 2002 national survey.* Washington DC: US Department of Justice, Office of Justice Programs, Bureau of Justice Statistics.

Eterno, J.A., Barrow, C.S., & Silverman, E.B. (2017). Forcible stops: Police and citizens speak out. *Public Administration Review*, 77(2). 181-192. doi:10.1111/puar.12684

El-Ghobashy, (2011). Minorities gain in NYPD ranks (2011, Jan 07). *Wall Street Journal* (Online) Retrieved from https://www.wsj.com/articles/SB10001424052748704415104576066302323002420

Evans, D.N., & Williams, C. (2017). Stop, question and frisk in New York City: A study of public opinions. *Criminal Justice Policy Review*, 28(7), 687-709. doi:10.1177/0887403415610166

Fagan, J., Geller, A., Davies, G. & West, V. (2010). Street stops and broken windows revisited: The demography logic of proactive policing in a safe and changing city. In S. Rice & M.D. White (Eds.) Race, ethnicity, and policing: New and essential readings. New York: New York University Press

Fagan, J., Tyler, T., & Meares, T. (2016). Street stops and police legitimacy in New York. In T. Delpeuch & J.E. Ross (Eds.). *Comparing the democratic governance of police intelligence: New models of participation and expertise in the United States and Europe.* (pp. 203-225). Retrieved from http://johnjay.jjay.cuny.edu/files/Fagan_Tyler_and_Meares_Street_Stops_and_Police_Le gitimacy_in_New_York.pdf

FBI Uniform Crime Report. (2012). *Crime in the U.S.—FBI.* Retrieved from https://ucr.fbi.gov/crime-in-the-u.s/2012

FBI Uniform Crime Report. (2017). *Crime in the U.S.—FBI.* Retrieved from https://ucr.fbi.gov/crime-in-the-u.s/2017

Ferrandino, J. (2015). Minority threat hypothesis and NYPD stop and frisk policy. *Criminal Justice Review,* 40(2), 209-229. doi:10.1177/0734016814564989

Flynn, E.A. (2016). Miranda and the evolution of policing. *Harvard Law & Policy Review,* 10, 101. Retrieved from ttps://heinonline.org/HOL/LandingPage?handle=hein.journals/harlpolrv10&div=10&id= &page=

Fradella, H.F., & White, M.D. (2017). Stop-and-frisk. *Academics advancing justice: A report on criminal justice reform.* Retrieved from http://academyforjustice.org/wp-content/uploads/2017/10/3_Reforming-Criminal-Justice_Vol_2_Stop-and-Frisk.pdf

Friedson, M., & Sharkey, P. (2015). Violence and neighborhood disadvantage after the crime decline. *The Annals of the American Academy,* 660(1), 341-358. doi:10.1177/0002716215579825

Fryer, R.G., Jr. (2018). Reconciling results on racial differences in police shootings. *Papers and Proceedings* (No. w24238), *National Bureau of Economic Research,* 1-6. doi:10.3386/w24238

Gelman, A., Fagan, J., & Kiss, A. (2007). An analysis of the New York City Police Department's "stop-and-frisk" policy in the context of claims of racial bias. *Journal of the American Statistical Association,* 102(479), 813-823. doi:10.1198/016214506000001040

Gerston, L.N. (2010). *Public Policy Making: Process and Principles.* London: Routledge.

Gerston, L.N. (2014). *Public policy making: Process and principles.* New York, NY: Routledge.

Goel, S., Rao, J.M., & Shroff, R. (2016). Precinct or prejudice? Understanding racial disparities in New York City's stop-and-frisk policy. *The Annals of Applied Statistics,* 10(1), 365-394. Retrieved from https://projecteuclid.org/euclid.aoas/1458909920

Goel, S., Perelman, M., Shroff, R., & Sklansky, D.A. (2017). Combatting police discrimination in the age of big data. *New Criminal Law Review,* 20(2). 181-132. doi:10.1525/nclr.2017.20.2.181

Greene, J.A. (1999). Zero tolerance: A case study of police policies and practices in New York City. *Crime & Delinquency,* 45(2), 171-187. doi:10.1177%2F0011128799045002001

Greene, J.C. (1994). Qualitative program evaluation: Practice and promise. In N. K. Denzin & A. S. Lincoln (Eds.), *Handbook of qualitative research*, (pp. 530-544). Thousand Oaks, CA: Sage.

Groff, E.R., Ratcliffe, J.H., Haberman, C.P., & Sorg, E.T. (2013). Foot Patrol in violent crime hot spots. *American Society of Criminology*, 51(1). doi:10.1111/j.1745-9125.2012.00290

Harcourt, B.E., & Ludwig, J. (2006). Broken windows: New evidence from New York City and a five-city social experiment. *University of Chicago Public Law Review*, 271-320. Retrieved from https://chicagounbound.uchicago.edu/cgi/viewcontent.cgi?article=2473&context=journal_articles

Head, B.W., & Alford, J. (2015). Wicked problems: Implications for public policy and management. *Administration & Society*, 47(6), 711-739. doi:10.1177%2F0095399713481601

Hemenway, D., & Solnick, S.J. (2015). The epidemiology of self-defense gun use: Evidence from the National Crime Victimization Surveys 2007-2011. *Preventive Medicine*, 79, 22-27. doi:10.1016/j.ypmed.2015.03.029

Howell, K.B. (2016). The costs of "broken windows" policing: Twenty years and counting. *City University of New York, 37 Cardozo Law Review*, 1059-1073. Retrieved from https://academicworks.cuny.edu/cgi/viewcontent.cgi?referer=https://scholar.google.com/&httpsredir=1&article=1123&context=cl_pubs

Huq, A.Z., Jackson, J., & Trinkner, R. (2017). Legitimating practices: Revisiting the predicates of policing legitimacy. *British Journal of Criminology*, 57(5), 1101-1122. doi:10.1093/bjc/azw037

Ibrahim, S., & Sidani, S. (2014). Strategies to recruit minority persons: A systematic review. *Journal of Immigrant and Minority Health*, 16(5), 882-888. doi:10.1007/s10903-013- 9783-y

John Jay College: databit202301.pdf (johnjayrec.nyc)

Jones-Brown, D., Gill, J., & Trone, J. (2010). Stop, question & frisk policing practices in New York City: A primer. *Center on Race, Crime and Justice, John Jay College of Criminal Justice*. Retrieved from https://static.prisonpolicy.org/scans/PRIMER_electronic_version.pdf

Jones-Brown, D., Stoudt, B.G., Johnston, B., & Moran, K. (2013). Stop, question & frisk policing practices in New York City: A primer. (Revised). *Center on Race, Crime and Justice, John Jay College of Criminal Justice*. Retrieved from http://www.atlanticphilanthropies.org/wp-content/uploads/2015/09/SQF_Primer_July_2013.pdf

Kamalu, N.C., & Onyeozili, E.C. (2018). A critical analysis of the "broken windows" policing in New York City and its impact: Implications for the criminal justice system and the African American community. *African Journal of Criminology and Justice Studies*, 11(1), 71-84. Retrieved from https://www.umes.edu/uploadedFiles/_WEBSITES/AJCJS/Content/VOL%2011%20KAMALU%20FINAL.pdf

Kang-Brown, J., Trone, J., Fratello, J., & Daftary-Kapur, T. (2013). *Generation later: What we've learned about zero tolerance in schools*. New York, NY: Vera Institute of Justice, Center of Youth Justice.

Keenan, D., & Thomas, T.M. (2014). An offense-severity model for stop-and-frisks. *The Yale Law Journal*, 123(5), 1448-1485. Retrieved from http://digitalcommons.law.yale.edu/cgi/viewcontent.cgi?article=5625&context=ylj

Kanno-Youngs, Z. (2017, Dec 27). NYPD program aims to build public trust --- but some critics say the department's community-policing effort has a wide gap to bridge. *Wall Street Journal.* Retrieved from https://www.wsj.com/articles/nypds-community-policing-aims- to-take-the-edge-off-crime-fighting-1514338810

Kenis, P., & Provan, K.G. (2009). Towards an exogenous theory of public network performance. *Public Administration*, 87(3), 440-456. doi.10.1111/j.1467- 9299.2009.01775.x

Kennedy, D.M. (2016). Is it any clearer? Generic qualitative inquiry and the VSAIEEDC model of data analysis. *The Qualitative Report*, 21(8), 1369-1379. Retrieved from https://nsuworks.nova.edu/tqr/vol21/iss8/1

Lincoln, Y.S., & Guba, E.G. (1985). *Naturalistic inquiry.* Beverly Hills, CA: Sage.

Lofstrom, M., & Raphael, S. (2016). Crime, the criminal justice system, and socioeconomic inequality. *Journal of Economic Perspectives*, 30(2), 103-126. doi:10.1257/jep.30.2.103

MacDonald, H. (2016). *The war on cops: How the attack on law and order makes everyone less safe.* New York, NY: Encounter Books.

MacDonald, J., Fagan, J., & Geller, A. (2016). The effects of local police surges on crime and arrests in New York City. *PLoS ONE*, 11(6), 1-9. doi:10.1371/journal.pone.0157223

Manski, C.F. & Nagin, D.S. (2017). Assessing benefits, costs, and disparate racial impacts of confrontational proactive policing. *PNAS*, 114(35), 9308-9313. doi:10.1073/pnas.1707215114

Mandell, M. & Keast, R. (2007). Evaluating network arrangements: Toward revised performance measures. *Public Performance & Management Review*, 30(4), 574-597. doi:10.2753/PMR1530-9576300406

Marsh, D. & McConnell, A. (2010). Towards a framework for establishing policy success. *Public Administration 88* (2), 564-583. doi:10.1111/j.1467-9299.2009.01803.x

McCandless, S.A. (2017). Social equity: A study of politics, management, and the equal protection of the law. (Unpublished doctoral dissertation). University of Colorado, Denver.

McConnell, A. (2010). Policy success, policy failure and grey areas in-between. *Journal of Public Policy*, 30(3), 345-362. doi:10.1017/S0143814X10000152

Meares, T.L. (2014). The law and social science of stop and frisk. *Annual Review of Law and Social Science*, 10, 335-352. doi:10.1146/annurev-lawsocsci-102612-134043

Meares, T.L. (2015). Programming errors: Understanding the constitutionality of stop-and-frisk as a program, not an incident. *Yale Law School Legal Scholarship Repository* (Paper 4921). (pp. 159-179). Retrieved from http://digitalcommons.law.yale.edu/fss_papers/4921

Morrow, W.J., White, M.D., & Fradella, H.F. (2017). After the stop: Exploring the racial/ethnic disparities in police use of force during *Terry* stops. *Police Quarterly*, 20(4), 367-396. doi:10.1177/1098611117708791

MSN News; https://www.msn.com/en-us/news/other/new-city-task-force-looks-to-address-parent-engagement-issues-youth-violence/ar-AA1oNhp3?ocid=BingNe

Nadal, K.L., & Davidoff, K.C. (2015). Perceptions of police scale (POPS): Measuring attitudes towards law enforcement and beliefs about police bias. *Journal of Psychology and Behavioral Science*, 3(2), 1-9. doi:10.15640/jpbs.v3b2al

Najdowski, C.J., Bottoms, B.L., & Goff, P.A. (2015). Stereotype threat and racial differences in citizens' experiences of police encounters. *Law and Human Behavior*, 39(5), 463-477. doi:10.1037/lhb0000140

National Research Council. (2004). Fairness and effectiveness in policing: The evidence. Washington, DC: National Academies Press.

New York Civil Liberties Union. (2018). *Stop Question and Frist Data*. Retrieved from https://www.nyclu.org/en/stop-and-Frisk-data

New York City Police Department. (2009). *Neighborhood policing*. Retrieved from www1.nyc.gov/site/nypd/bureaus/patrol/neighborhood-coordination-officers.page

New York City Police Department. (2016). *The New York City Police Department (NYPD) sworn officers*. Retrieved from www1.nyc.gov/site/nypd/bureaus/patrol/neighborhood- coordination-officers. Page

Neyroud, P.W. (2017). Balancing public safety and individual rights in street policing. *Commentary for Proceedings of the National Academy of Sciences*, 114(35), 9231-9233. doi:10.1073/pnas.1712541114

Oya, A.S. (2006). The cultural diversity phenomenon in organizations and different approaches for effective cultural diversity management: A literary review. *Cross Cultural Management*, 13(4), 296-315. doi.org/10.1108/13527600610713404

National Crime Victimization Survey; NCVS Dashboard: Home (ojp.gov)

Pare, P. (2014). Indicators of police performance and their relationships with homicide rates across 77 nations. *International Criminal Justice Review*, 24(3), 254-270. doi:10.1177/1057567714548453

Patterson, C.V. (2017). NYPD Application of stop, question, and frisk: Effects on citizens attitudes towards the police and police Community relations. Retrieved from ProQuest Dissertations Publishing (No. 10643127).

Percy, W.H., Kostere, K., & Kostere, S. (2015). Generic qualitative research in psychology. *The Qualitative Report*, 20(2), 76-85. Retrieved from https://nsuworks.nova.edu/tqr/vol20/iss2/7

Platzer, H. & James, T. (1997). Methodological issues conducting sensitive research on lesbian and gay men's experience of nursing care. *Journal of Advanced Nursing*, 25(3), 626-633. doi:10.1046/j.1365-2648.1997.t01-1-1997025626.x

Politifact; https://www.politifact.com/article/2007/sep/01/how-much-credit-giuliani-due-fighting-crime/

President's Task Force on 21st Century Policing. (2015). *Final report of the President's task force on 21st century policing*. Washington, DC. Office of Community Oriented Policing Services.

Pyrooz, D.C., Decker, S.H., Wolfe, S.E., & Shjarback, J.A. (2016). Was there a Ferguson effect on crime rates in large U.S. cities? *Journal of Criminal Justice*, 46, 1-8. doi:10.1016/j.jcrimjus.2016.01.001

Ray, J.M. (2014). *Rethinking community policing*. Retrieved from https://ebookcentral-proquest-com.library.capella.edu

Rengifo, A.F., & Fowler, K. (2016). Stop, question, and complain: Citizen grievances against the NYPD and the opacity of police stops across New York City precincts, 2007–2013. *Journal of Urban Health*, 93(1), 32-41. doi:10.1007/s11524-015-0010-0

Reynoso, L.F.L., & Tovar, L.A. (2014). Organizational variables in effectiveness of police. *International Review of Management and Business Research*, 3(2), 827-846. Retrieved from https://www.researchgate.net/profile/Luis_Arturo_Rivas_Tovar/publication/280720599_Organizational_Variables_in_Effectiveness_of_Police/links/55c280d008aeca747d5dd0e3.pdf

Rice, S.K. & White, M.D. (Eds.) (2010). *Race, ethnicity and policing: New and essential readings*. New York, NY: New York University Press.

Ridgeway, G, (2007). Analysis of racial disparities in the New York Police Department's stop, question, and frisk practices. *Rand Corporation*. Retrieved from https://www.rand.org/pubs/technical_reports/TR534.html

Robertiello, G. (Ed.). (2018). *The use and abuse of police power in America: Historical milestones and current controversies*. Santa Barbara, CA: ABC-CLIO.

Rohe, W.M., Adams, R.E., & Arcury, T.A. (2001). Community policing and planning. American Planning Association. *Journal of the American Planning Association*, 67(1), 78-90. doi:10.1080/01944360108976357

Rosenfeld, R. & Fornango, R. (2014). The impact of police stops on precinct robbery and burglary rates in New York City, 2003-2010. *Justice Quarterly*, 31(1), 96-122. doi:10.1080/07418825.2012.712152

Rosenfeld, R., & Fornango, R. (2017). The relationship between crime and stop, question, and frisk rates in New York City neighborhoods. *Justice Quarterly*, 34(6), 931-951. doi:10.1080/07418825.2016.1275748

Rosenfeld, R., Terry, K., & Chauhan, P. (2014). New York's crime drop puzzle: Introduction to the special issue. *Justice Quarterly*, 31(1), 1-4. doi:10.1080.07418825.2012.754923

Royse, D., Thyer, B., & Padgett, D. (2014). *Program Evaluation: An introduction to an evidence-based approach* (6th ed.). Boston, MA: Cengage Learning.

Schultz, D., & Vile, J.R. (2004). *The encyclopedia of civil liberties in America.* doi.org/10.4324/9781315699868

Sewell, A.A., & Jefferson, K.A. (2016). Collateral damage: The health effects of invasive police encounters in New York City. *Journal of Urban Health*, 93(1). doi:10.1007/s11524-015-0016-7

Sewell, A.A., Jefferson, K.A., & Lee, H. (2016). Living under surveillance: Gender, psychological distress, and stop-question-and-frisk policing in New York City. *Social Science & Medicine*, 159, 1-13. doi:10.1016/j.socscimed.2016.04.024

Sorg, E. T., Haberman, C. P., Ratcliffe, J. H., & Groff, E. R. (2013). Foot patrol in violent crime hot spots: The longitudinal impact of deterrence and posttreatment effects of displacement. *Criminology*, 51(1), 65-101. doi:10.1111/j.1745-9125.2012.00290.x

Streeton, R., Cooke, M., & Campbell, J. (2004). Researching the researchers: Using a showballing technique. *Nurse Researcher*, 12(1), 35-46. Retrieved from EBSCOhost (14502363).

Sweeten, G. (2016). What works, what doesn't, what's constitutional? The problem with assessing unconstitutional police practice. *Criminology & Public Policy*, 15(1), 67-73. doi:10.1111/1745-9133.12176

Vile, J.R. (2010). *Essential Supreme Court decisions: summaries of leading cases in US constitutional law.* Rowman & Littlefield Publishers.

Thomas, D.R. (2006). A general inductive approach for analyzing qualitative evaluation data. *American Journal of Evaluation*, 27(2), 237-246. doi:10.1177%2F1098214005283748

Trinkner, R., Tyler, T.R., Goff, P.A., & Atiba, P. (2016). Justice from within: The relations between procedurally just organizational climate and police organizational efficiency, endorsement of democratic policing, and officer well-being. *Psychology, Public Policy, and Law*, 22(2), 158-172. doi:10.1037/law0000085

Tseloni, A., Mailley, J., Farrell, G., & Tilley, N. (2010). Exploring the international decline in crime rates. *European Journal of Criminology*, 7(5), 375-394. doi:10.1177/1477370810367014

Tyler, T.R., Goff, P.A., & MacCoun, R.J. (2015). The impact of psychological science on policing in the United States: Procedural justice, legitimacy, and effective law enforcement. *Psychological Science in the Public Interest*, 16(3), 75-109. doi:10.1177/1529100615617791

U.S. Census, 2017

Ward, S.F. (2014). Stopping stop and frisk. *ABA Journal*, 100, 38-45. Retrieved from http://search.proquest.com.library.capella.edu/docview/1506936746?accountid=27965

Wargo, W.G. (2015). *Identifying assumptions and limitations for your dissertation*. Menifee, CA: Academic Information Centre.

Weisburd, D., & Eck, J.E. (2004). What can police do to reduce crime, disorder, and fear? *Annals of the American Academy AAPSS*, 593(1), 42-65. doi:10.1177/0002716203262548

Weisburd, D., Telep, C.W., & Lawton, B.A. (2014). Could innovations in policing have contributed to the New York City crime drop even in a period of declining police strength? The case of stop, question, and frisk as a hot spots policing strategy. *Justice Quarterly*, 31(1), 129-153. doi:10.1080/07418825.2012.754920

Weisburd, D., Wooditch, A., Weisburd, S., & Yang, S.M. (2016). Do Stop, Question, and Frisk Practices Deter Crime? *Criminology & Public Policy*, 15(1), 31-56. doi:10.1111/1745- 9133.12172

Weiss, D.B., Santos, M.R., Testa, A., & Kumar, S. (2016). The 1990s homicide decline: A western world or international phenomenon? A research note. *Homicide Studies*, 20(4), 321-334. doi:10.1177/1088767916634406

Welsh, B.C., Braga, A.A., & Bruinsma, G. J. (2015). Reimagining broken windows: From theory to policy. *Journal of Research in Crime and Delinquency*, 52(4), 447-463. doi:10.1177/0022427815581399

White, M.D. (2011). The New York City police department, its crime-control strategies, and organizational changes, 1970-2009. *Justice Quarterly*, 31(1), 74-95. doi:10.1080/07418825.2012.723032

White, M.D., & Fradella, H.F. (2016). *Stop and frisk: The use and abuse of a controversial policing tactic*. New York, NY: New York University Press.

White, M.D., Fradella, H.F., Morrow, W.J., & Mellom, D. (2016). Federal civil litigation as an instrument of police reform: A natural experiment exploring the effects of the *Floyd* ruling on stop-and-frisk activities in New York City. *Ohio St Journal of Criminal Law*, 14, 1-58. Retrieved from https://kb.osu.edu/bitstream/handle/1811/79759/OSJCL_V14N1_009.pdf?sequence=1

Wieringa, R.J. (2014). Design science methodology for information systems and software engineering. Heidelberg, The Netherlands, Springer.

Wildavsky, A. (2017). *Speaking truth to power: Art and craft of policy analysis*. New York, NY: Routledge.

Wilson, J.Q., & Kelling, G.L. (1982). Broken windows. *The Atlantic Online*. Retrieved from http://www.theatlantic.com/doc/print/198203/broken-windows

Worden, R.E., McLean, S.J. (2018). Measuring, managing, and enhancing procedural justice in policing: promise and pitfalls. *Criminal Justice Policy Review*, 29(2), 149-171. doi:10.1177/0887403416662505

Zimring, F.E. (2012). The city that became safe: New York's lessons for urban crime and its control. New York, NY: Oxford University Press.

About the Author

Dr. Richard Vargus has spent his life in service to his country and community. Serving forty years in the Armed Forces of the Unites States, and various positions in Federal, and local law enforcement. His military service includes tours in Iraq and Afghanistan. He is a graduate of the Air War College and holds a Doctorate in Public Administration. He has been recognized for his service with multiple awards and decorations, to include the Bronze Star. Dr. Vargus currently resides with his wife Norma, a decorated Iraqi veteran herself, in New York.